A NARRATIVE TALE OF

MOROCCO

J PETER HALL

To order additional copies of this book, contact:
Xlibris
844-714-8691
www.Xlibris.com
Orders@Xlibris.com

ISBN:	Softcover	978-1-7960-9287-5
	Hardcover	978-1-6641-4607-5
	EBook	978-1-7960-9286-8

Print information available on the last page.

Rev. date: 12/17/2020

This is for Thomas F. Duffy, my first teacher of Literature at Massachusetts Maritime Academy, a class in which every week we students presented our new discourse. By Mr. Duffy, we were birds with not only our cages open, but given wings that can fly in space. Those who teach from within, are never “the late”.

Tourist group from Sao Paulo, Brazil to Casablanca, Morocco Jane Zatoni-Hall and J. Peter Hall

IN NOVEMBER 2013

Over a year earlier in 2012, Zhäné (that is how Jane sounds in Portuguese, and how it is tattooed on my right arm) had been looking into tourists for Istanbul, but it was not being considered friendly at that time; it was put on the back burner. Then in October 2013, that same travel agent sent a brochure of Morocco. With nine nights at three different hotels, bus with tourist guide, a list of all the cities to be investigated, with breakfast and supper in the price there had to be a catch. Upon discussion in their office, we learned it was on the up, and so we paid right then.

After packing on Sunday evening, the call from our receptionist at 2:00 AM, and again at 2:25 for that the agreed taxi man had just arrived made us feel clever with having had a two-hour nap. Driving to any airport at 2:30 AM on Monday has one flying to the airport. Arriving at the required 03:00 AM and finding our check-in—one need not be a detective when it is the only one open—we became the caboose of a long train. By 07:00 AM, we were in the air. Flying east can be called "against the current," for our arriving at Casablanca showed a sunless city.

We all shuffled over to the buses—company Caravan—and by saying our names, we were told which of the buses numbered 3, 4, or 5; we settled in the back of bus number 3.

Making no change of clothes after dropping off our suitcases up on the fifth floor, we entered the cafeteria down below with a half a dozen already in. The food was good, and by the time I rose for second helpings, the place was packed. This hunter was focusing on certain items that could not be placed on top of the mounded first plate. It was only when heading back to our table that my eyes were up. After three hours in the airport, ten hours in the plane, another hour at the landing airport, and thirty minutes on the bus, I expected to see a familiar face or two. I not only saw none, but the clothing—though not from a wedding—looked more presentable than that of us, the experienced long fliers, relaxed with big pockets. We smoothly slipped out after our second plate and found *our* cafeteria.

Back upstairs and looking out our window, the fog showed only the three-floored building across the street. Seeing no light past it, I assumed that this low price landed us in the outskirts of the city. In the morning, I saw the beach of Casablanca just beyond that building.

On the bus that morning, we drove up the hill to look at many mansions. I used that word not for the size of the houses, nor their land—only twenty feet from house to house—but their impressive elaborate detail; synonym to Rolls-Royce and Lamborghini, where it is price, not size. Millenniums ago, when exploring by boat or horse, a king would hire a painter or drafter to explain the new territories. This is my first day of my first time on a tourist trip, and I must use that as my excuse for not having my camera on my possession for the showing of those little mansions.

Driving down the hill and into the city, we saw buildings no more than six or seven floors in height. And all these buildings—be they apartment, hotel, business office—their ground floor is a restaurant, store, café.

COMPTABILITE
CAFÉ RESTAURANT

This picture is from our hotel bedroom. A great number of red lights in this city are the way as seen here, with a rotary, all with grass and palm trees. Rotary though they are, they are all red-light and only green-light with their opposite lane. Many intersections are the arrival of six streets, a web. There are some not a small circle, but a 100 or 200 ft. long rectangular park.

I spoke of cafes. Café is strictly male, where they smoke hashish, play cards, and drink mint tea. "Cannabis is grown in the North East of Morocco for centuries. But the casual use by a goat herd has been overtaken by multi-million dollar industry."- from Wikipedia

This is a very chic church; its age I did not look into. There are no windows seen from the outside. But that wall is an ivory tower, a certain distance out from the glass in order to give it light to the 150-ft.-long glasses on both left and right side.

جهة
الدارالبيضاء الكبرى
REGION
DU GRAND CASABLANCA

This is one of the sixteen administrations of this department in Morocco. It covers the whole block. The picture below shows some very intricate carving on the wall above the tiles. They are not carvings, but the grinding of marble to make it "sand," and then together with some liquid to form as you wish before it hardens.

This window on "Main St.," Casablanca, shows regular ladies' coatdresses, whereas those seen outside show more elaborate apparel, and using their own scarf, while others use the hood that is a part of the coatdress. Some of the purses shown on the display look like briefcases, which reminds me of a lady at a different location walking on the opposite side of the street, all dressed in black from head to shoes, with a briefcase, walking as a Sergeant in the Army, while talking on her cell phone.

In the afternoon, we arrived at Hassan II Mosque. We walked around the area—our appointment of entrance being not until our day of farewell from Morocco, eight days later. In Islam, "the Throne of Allah was built on water," hence the reason this mosque was built beyond the beach. Commenced on July 12, 1986, and completed in 1993, the construction was three years with 1,200 men around the clock, and soon into the work, and then to completion, six thousand tradition Moroccan artisans for five years. Two large breakwaters were also built, to protect the mosque from erosive action of the ocean waves, which can be up to ten meters (33 feet) in height. The walls are of handcrafted marble. The marble floors are always warm, for all the shoeless feet. The seabed is visible through the glass floor of the building's hall below. Also below are the Turkish Baths. In the minaret of this mosque, there is a laser pointing directly to Mecca; Mecca is the city where Muhammad was born.

Hassan II Mosque holds twenty-five thousand people, eight thousand of them being women on the mezzanines, left and right. This mosque was built to withstand earthquake.

Here is the seabed, the area of the Turkish bath. As I was settling in the area of one of these water users—not in use—I saw not the two-inch ebb below the floor. The tattoo on my left hip subsided in a month, but the camera was open at the time, its lenses bent five degrees. Had that been the first day, the 567 pictures would be a smaller number.

After some time, we drove a mile south to a café by the beach. It was not the espresso that had us walking to the hotel—for it being only a few blocks—but a longer time for strolling along an empty boardwalk.

In the early evening, there was a meeting in one of the convention rooms of the hotel. Our friend Giselda Micchaelo has been a tourist guide for ten years. It was only her free time that moment that had her able to join us. But her free time was for looking into and confirming Internet commercials of Morocco. And of us, one hundred passengers who flew from Sao Paulo, Brazil to Casablanca, Morocco, over a third were as is Giselda, but some freelance, some family companies—all of those with the wife in charge—and some being part of a larger company.

From Wikipedia: "Tourism is the second largest foreign exchange earner in Morocco, after the phosphate industry. The Morocco Government is heavily invested in tourism development. A new tourism strategy called 'Vision 2010' was developed after the accession of King Mohammed VI in [23 July] 1999."

This "Vision" was a speech given by Mohammed VI on January 10, 2001, in Marrakech: A National Meeting on Tourism.

As Mick Jagger was accepted to the London School of Economics at seventeen years of age and completed that college before making the seen in the United States, Mohammed VI finished law school 15 years later at age twenty-two, with his research paper dealt with "The Arab-African Union and the Strategy of the Kingdom of Morocco in Matters of International Relations." Of many distinctions as rising, Mohammed VI trained in Brussels with Jacques Delors, then president of the European Commission. Mohammed VI obtained his PhD in law with distinction on October 29, 1993, from the French University of Nice Sofia Antipolis.

Both Mick Jagger and Mohammed VI are rather similar to American Football Quarterbacks up until the mid-nineteen-seventies, wherein they need no guidance from the coach, play to play.

The next morning, our well-filled stomachs settled into our now owned seats of the bus number 3. We drove straight south to the city Marrakech. Zhane's and my cameras were not present at the time, so allow my description to suffice. The land on either side of the highway was dry, but strange in my eyes for it is all stones and rocks, some heavy by hand but most smaller than half an inch. The shrubs there were four feet high by four feet wide, scattered about, one hundred feet apart. Every few miles we saw a group of sheep—fifteen to thirty—not always with a shepherd, a much smaller number of goats following with them.

Now here, I must make an intuitive conjecture: There is hardly enough food and water for these ruminating herbivores. It could be they receive all their food at the stable, and do their walking for blood flow, chewing over in the sun, all with no carnivores.

As arriving into Marrakech, we saw a new city. Just a few turns from our southern route and we were escorted down Hotel Boulevard. While rising to store our suitcases in our rooms, in the back we saw outside tables, barbecues, tennis, and a reservoir over a mile in circumference.

Marrakech was inhabited by Berber farmers since Neolithic times, 4,000 to 10,000 BC. The west side of the Sahara had richer plants 20,000 BC, and so there is no reason to refuse the thought of the Berbers being there for 200,000 years—so close to our birth place. In history, Morocco is within a larger area west of Egypt. Artifacts of the Berber people are seen throughout Libya, Tunisia, Algeria, Morocco, and Mauritania. Cave paintings have been found in southern Algeria. That old part of City Marrakech will be seen tomorrow. Right now we go to Fantasy Restaurant!

All groups in this event are out at the gate welcoming our entrance, all fifteen men on horses, waiters, dancers, instrument users. The name Fantasy Restaurant is not required for we are already there. We continue our walk out to the arena. The rectangular sandfield is football size, with a wooden board all around it.

For us city boys, the feeling of a rifle is new.

A short time surveying the grounds had us following the one passage into the four tents that run parallel to the coliseum. There are circular tables on both sides, good for eight or nine wolves. You'll see shortly the reason for that.

We were given a tasty appetite, and then the big plate with a whole lamb. The eight of us on our table did our best trying to finish it.

After the feast, several ladies arrived with the men and their instruments. Two of the ladies were belly dancers, who allowed money to be wrapped under their belt, or bra. After the end of the time inside, we all strolled out, gathering at the side of the fairground, laughing. Every table had a story to tell. On a whim, five of the horses galloped from their repose at the far end. "Arabian Horse—one of a breed of horses raised in Arabia, noted for their speed." The land of Arabia is half desert, and the hooves of horses from that region have adapted for that; in this sandy yard they are right at home. If you look at the pictures on page 11, you will agree they are Arabian horses. And that is all said in order for you to believe me when I say that they took off like greyhounds. As these racers flew past us, their equestrians fired their "cannons." Right after that, a second batch of five horses took off. Needless to say, they had our attention this time. The third and final, and then we walked to the bus, all the workers on both side, as upon arriving.

Thursday morning had us driving directly to the fair in the center of Marrakech. This city is a "coconut palm tree," with its heart of palm in the center.

This archway, not in the bus, but some height.

The café from where we sat is located to the right of the picture above.

Shopping! - Zhane

We are in Morocco, but those hats here in Marrakech are not the usual brimless hat with a felt tossed out of the center of the top. Google shows this type of hat for winter, and this being mid-November, and they're not kids…

Here you see Arabic and French language. Of several arrivals through the centuries, France was the last Protectorate from 1912 until 1956. All the street signs show their names thusly.

French and English. They are on the same street. Maybe a new owner living strictly on tourists.

Stores having a crescent displayed outside tell you of their fluent use of Arabic language. (This picture was actually made in Casablanca.)

We are soon to enter a greater number of emporiums inside.

The oldest area of barter and market is covered. I failed to make pictures of any inside part of this elaborate, "small intestine"—bring your compass! In the center, things opened up to display the King's Home, a private hide away that was made public by the French.

The picture on the next page has one first infer that's Peter at the bar. But second look shows rugs behind me. This location is actually when we are in a large, two-floored store before entering the enclosed market. Somewhere close to the King's House, we rose two flights of stairs to enter the arena of the pharmacist. The room is about twenty-five square feet, with the audience sitting on chairs all around the walls, and a smaller row close to the lecturer in the center. Between the two groups of people, there is an open seven feet walkway. All of the medicines presented are from Mother Earth, not man-made. His three assistants walked around with samples for all of us to see and smell, have it rubbed on the forearm. One of the spectators in the center was a bald man, and the pharmacist rubbed one of his samples on that baldhead, for good luck. After about an hour and a half—all taking notes—we all walked into the other room for buying.

This is looking back upon our exit from the King's House.

Here we are on Friday morning driving straight west to the Atlantic, and this here is just the outskirts of Marrakech, not yet in the desert.

As can be seen in the background of the picture above and the young ones in the picture below, the olives are in good shape. But as we go farther away from the rivers and rain, the olive will be no more. But there is a cousin that lives almost as a cactus, and you will see shortly.

The rocky desert to the west of Morocco is the same as we saw when driving from the north, but with a great difference: the houses—they being a half a mile to a mile apart—are in a three acres oasis, with not just palm trees, but also deep plants rising up from dark, green grass. November is in the dry season; the bridges we crossed showed dry rivers, all rocks on the bed, though most of them larger than those on the terrain of Moroccan sheep. Ten miles before arriving at the Port Essaouira, we pulled over to take pictures of an Argan tree.

From Wikipedia: "Argan—eight to ten meters (25–31 ft.) in height, 150 to 200 years old. They are thorny, with gnarled trunks. The leaves on the edge of the desert are small, 2–4 cm. long, flowers also small too. The fruit with a thick bitter peel surrounding a sweet-smelling but unpleasantly flavored layer of pulpy pericarp. This surrounds the very hard nut, which contains one (occasionally two or three) small oil-rich seeds. The fruit takes over a year to mature, ripening in June or July, when black and dry. Until this happens, goats are kept out of the argan woodlands by wardens. Goats seem to enjoy the leaves and fruits, the nuts are dropped for gathering."

Soon by, we pulled over to the farm shop that allows one to walk by and observe the ladies doing the most labor-intensive part of oil-extraction, removing the soft pulp (used to feed animals) and the cracking by hand, between two stones of the hard nut.

From Wikipedia: "The seeds are then removed and gently roasted. This roasting accounts for part of the oil's distinctive, nutty flavor. Argan oil is used for dipping bread, on couscous, salads, and similar uses. The unroasted oil is traditionally used as a treatment for skin diseases and has become flavored by European cosmetics manufacturers. Argan, a tree requiring little water, is also grown in Negev, Israel, and Arabah."

This is an extremely tough job these ladies are doing, and this picture above is a moment after the priceless smile she gave me.

After the cognizance, Zhane bought some creams and unroasted oil. I bought two plates over a foot in diameter.

Our final destination of the day was Essaouira. This bay has been occupied since prehistoric times. We have found, and carbon dated boats there of 10,000 BC. There are two good reasons for settling there: the temperature and the fish. “The average temperature change of only 5°C (9°F) between summer and winter.” The main reason for the second statement is the variety of fish.

We parked our bus on the northeast side of this town and walked southwest to the pier; mind you, this place is a maze, with many passage lanes that are actually streets.

We all know actor Orson Welles. In 1952, he was the actor and director of his classic version of "Othello." His themes contained several memorable shots in the "labyrinthine streets and alleyways" in Essaouira. There is a bust of Welles located close to the sea, and learning the time of that bust could tell us more its reason. In the late 1960s, Essaouira became a hippie hangout. Cat Stevens spent some time here, Jimi Hendricks, Brian Jones, to name a few.

As Colorado's sky is for painters, so Mali's and Mauritania's sound is for listeners, with certain dances, Gnawa healing rituals, though their magical treatments must have the required formula to help a scorpion sting. And as Colorado focused on Santa Fe, the Gnawas focused on Essaouira in 1998, with Gnawa Festival of World Music, normally in the last week of June. It lasts four days and attracts annually around 450,000 spectators, dubbed as the "Moroccan Woodstock." It includes also rock, jazz, and reggae.

When spreading out in AD 632, the Arabs brought more than just their Islam, but also their knowledge, tools, tiles, and much more.

Soon after this area, we slipped into one of the enclosed shops. But rather than as the enrapturing snake in Marrakech, we continued straight south-south-west. I imagine that the two-hundred- to threehundred-yard exit was visible—so unbent was the channel—and that the only reason for myself not seeing that fact was the alluring of most of the stores as we passed. Indeed, the very first shop sold many one-hundred-year-old boat lights. Those lights are all intricate, thick glass of green or red, over a foot in height, eight inches in diameter. There were all kinds of other boat lights and memorabilia, for use, or display. These lights I speak of shall be on both sides of my fireplace mantel. And I shall buy two sets, one for my friend Bill Grindle. Out of High School, Bill and I drove his van from Brookline, Massachusetts down to Daytona Beach, Florida. We worked on a fishing boat. Two extra men whose only sleeping was up on the floor of the lookout tower. The calm nights were deceiving, for in the morning upon waking, I did my usual jump right up. But the windy, wavy mornings gave the boat her "wake-up," which had me air-bound, landing on the four feet high wall, every morning.

Later, both of us were on different vessels, and then after that on different licenses on land. But the eyes will always see the sea, like the salt, and with these lights on the mantel, feeling not at anchor. Call it a mission, but I weakly kept up with the crowd, instead of doing some bargaining and buying those lights. So now I must make amends, to rectify.

Here we are close to our day's restaurant. No hamburgers there!

This green roof was our exit from the enclosed shops.

From Wikipedia: "In 1506, the King of Portugal, D. Manuel I, ordered a fortress to be built in Essaouira, named Castelo Real de Mogador. In 1510 the fortress of Mogador fell to the local resistance of the Regraga Fraternity four years after it was established. During the 16th century, powers including Spain, England, the Netherlands, and France tried in vain to conquer the locality. Essaouira remained a haven for the export of sugar, molasses, and the anchoring of pirates."

Here is island Mogador as looking from the beach of Essaouira. The fortress is on the perfect point of the land, not this named island.

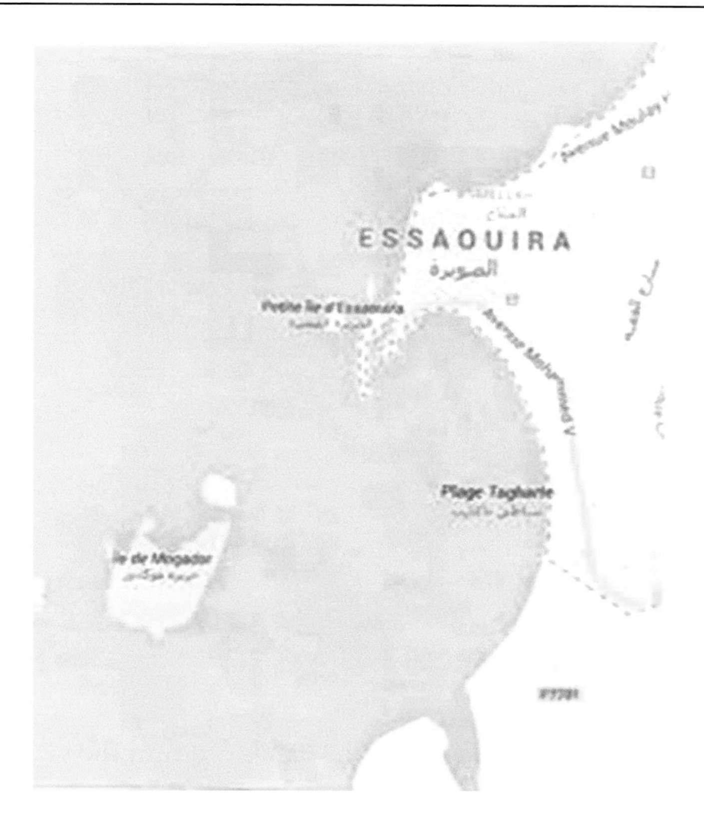

On page 26, I spoke of the finding of boats in this bay that were dated from 10,000 BC. The fishermen docked here for the blocking of the waves, yet close to the highway of fish that circulate from the equator. That warm water does not all turn south upon arriving in Europe; and that is why St. Ives, England and Tralee, Ireland never lose their value, and why Norway sells sardines.

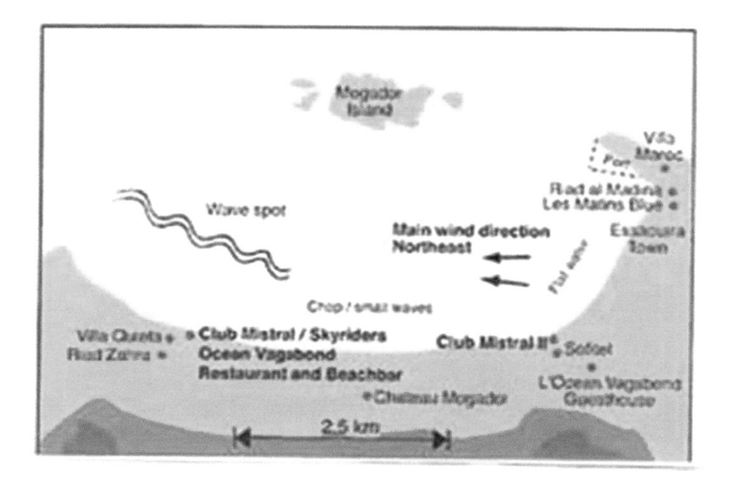

Though Essaouira is a yearly event in June for the gathering of musical instruments, it is a weekend event all year long for kite surfing and wind surfing. Our arrival at this bay was on a Friday midafternoon. Had it been on Saturday, these picture would have been from my camera.

Kite surfing. Notice the belt holds the kite, while the hands can turn the kite.

Windsurfing. I see a competition for the title by height.

During our late lunch on the fish pier of Essaouira, we discussed the city of Agadir, the next big port south of this one. We were told of the great earthquake of February 29, 1960, which killed one third of the forty thousand people. The Richter scale of 5.7 was deceiving for that it was right below the city, for a solid fifteen seconds. A great number of the buildings constructed between 1945 and 1955 were not up to par with the code—the right material, bracing, etc.—and they dropped like a flat tire. They seemed to have forgotten their own earthquake of 1731.

Both Agadir and Essaouira are in good geographic location; the same year when Morocco took back Essaouira from Portugal, Agadir was "a town of some notoriety. The name 'Agadir' is a common Berber noun Agadir, meaning 'wall enclosure, fortified building, citadel'. There are many more towns in Morocco called Agadir. (This) city of Agadir's full name in Tashelhit is Agadir n Yighir, literally 'the fortress of the cape'." In 1572, the Casbah [some call it Kasbah] was built on the top of the hill of Agadir. The 1731 earthquake damaged much, but not the Kasbah, the fortress, lookout, café tower. The Sultan had the goods relocated to Essaouira. Fifteen years later, Dutch set up trading post at the foot of the Kasbah, under the authority of the Sultan. Business went well for fifteen years, but then it declined because of the pre-eminence given to the competing port of Essaouira by the Sultan, a punishment for rebuilding without his authority. By 1789 it was called a ghost town, a few houses. This decline lasted a century and a half, and only reopened in 1881 by the Sultan of that time—and timing—to supply the expedition he planned in the south. It was only given the OK, for by 1884 it was still called "a poor village, depopulated and without trade." By 1899, France wanted Protectorate of Morocco—the almost final land of Africa that was not owned by Europe. By 1905, France needed to be "renounced any remaining interest in Egypt." Tangier, Morocco is the City on the entrance of the Mediterranean.

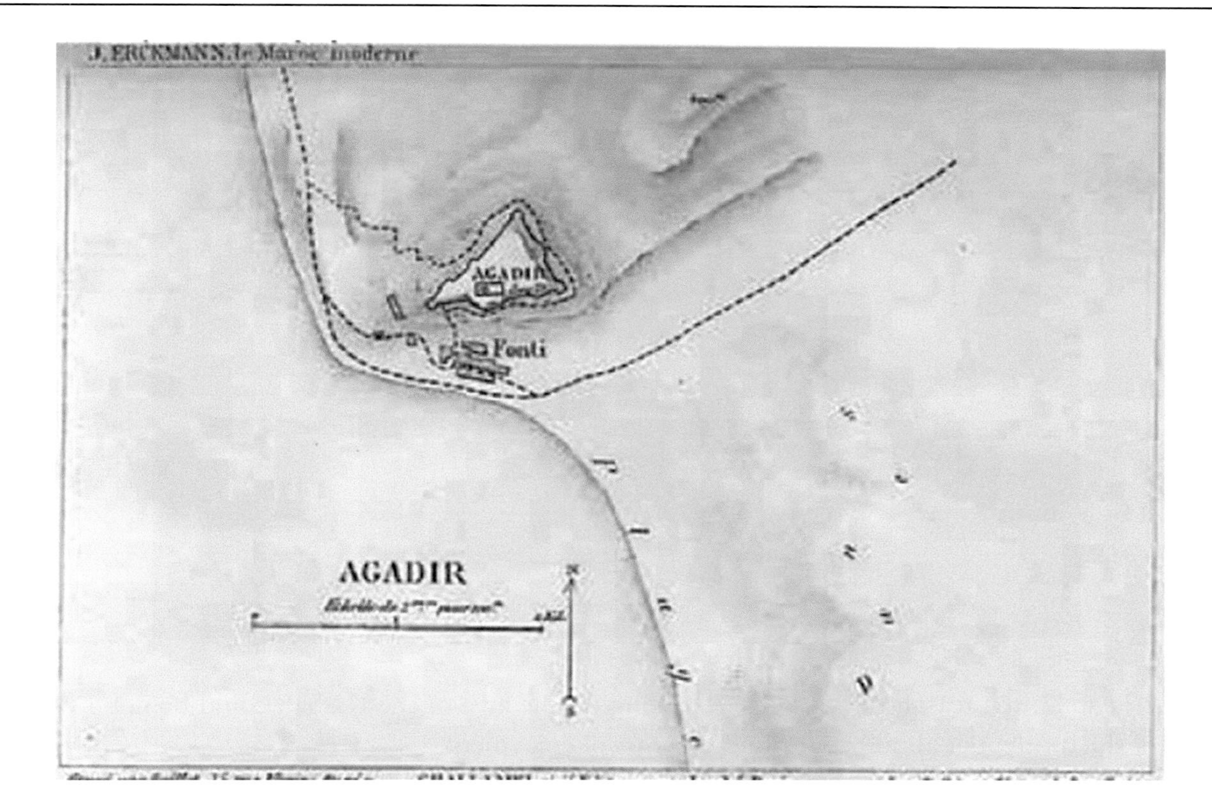

Germany wanted Tangier and Agadir, and it almost "broke the camel's back" when France finally got Morocco in 1912. In the next forty-eight years, Agadir grew well to forty thousand people. After the second earthquake, Agadir grew exponentially to 609,088 people.

Agadir. This beach is six miles (10K) long.

Agadir and Essaouira are two examples of a great number of names of locations that are native Berber word, similar to Chicago, Illinois, Massachusetts…

Made in 1572, the reason for no longer building on the area of the Kasbah could be not a worry or concern of the future, but almost four hundred years of enjoyment.

The Saadian Tombs in Marrakech date back from the time of Sultan Ahman al-Mansur, 1578–1603. The Tombs were discovered in 1917 and were restored by Beaux-Arts Service.

Saturday we drove straight south-east to Ouarzazatte. The map on page 34 will show you of our need to drive over the Atlas Mountains. This was a day of bus changing, for our bus number 3 was on the way to the desert—to each their own. When we got down at 08:07, bus number 4 was already gone, quite different from bus number 3. We asked for the bus to be called and to return, claiming of Peter's diarrhea that morning, but that myth did not work. He agreed to stop for some time. So by taxi we were there in a flash, and here is where it starts to become interesting.

As I was paying the taxi, Zhane entered the verbal arena outside of the bus. The vexatious lady would not stop, no matter how diplomatic Zhane spoke. The lady's husband started in on it as I arrived, and we just brushed them off, entering into a bus full of smiling people. What goes around comes around? A short jump ahead to Wednesday, our day to the airport; we were back on bus number 3, but we learned from first hand this story: When leaving the hotel to arrive at the airport, the driver of bus number 4 was doing quite a bit of honking, pushing his agitated way from the parking lot. There happened to be a police in sight, and in sound. The cop walked over to the bus and had the bus driver's license taken away from him. It was one thing to do something else for the day, but needing to go to the airport is another matter. The driver spoke to the guide man, who spoke to his manager; the manager spoke with the hotel manager, the hotel manager called the mayor, the mayor called the governor, the governor called the chief of police, and then the bus driver was given a one day license ticket to allow him to go to the airport.

Now we are back to Saturday. We drove straight south without interruption to the high part of a few of the many mountains in the area. So clear a day that as we see ants and termites climbing upward, so seemed the trucks or buses from two or three miles away, the usual curves of a mountain's road where those large vehicles stop to allow their comrade to do the turn. While driving from Boston to Toronto, and using Route 90, Massachusetts has the Green Mountains, and then New York State has the Appalachian Plateau, where certain parts have a sign "Falling Rocks Ahead." I say that to compare with the higher parts of the Atlas Mountains. They too have "suicidal" rocks! And with the road so close to the mountain's epidermis, I felt we were running the gauntlet!

Here we are not yet in that great height. Marrakech receives the same constant wind from the north as does Essaouira. And you will see that confirmed as we land over this mountain.

Here we are in Ouarzazate, a Berber camp for thousands of years, mostly a place for storage for the jaunt to Marrakech. With the French auspice, they blossomed in to a small town. This studio you see here, the earliest movie filming I found on the Internet was 1962, Lawrence of Arabia; 1975, The Man Who Would Be King; 1988, The Last Temptation of Christ; 2000, Gladiator; and 2013, Atlantis. And these are only a small example of a constant flow of movies made here. The most important reason is the clear, blue sky, and so movies being set and finished in short order.

As these two Egyptian men stand still, look at the fence closer to you from their feet, and then consider their height.

As walking around, we see props of different time and stature.

Across the street, we were welcomed by a native of this town. He led us throughout this large house that was previously owned by a rich man, an extra room for his mistress. One room had a seventy-year-old ceiling of palm tree. Another room had a ceiling of intricate wood held with egg and plaster.

The Studio is outside of the town Ouarzazate. I spoke on page 37 of the enlargement of this town after the French Protectorate. Almost all the people here are Berber, and what was one is now many Kasbahs.

As seeing the use of metal on this Kasbah, one concludes this being not from eternity, but one of a more recent age.

Within, all the making and selling of rugs…

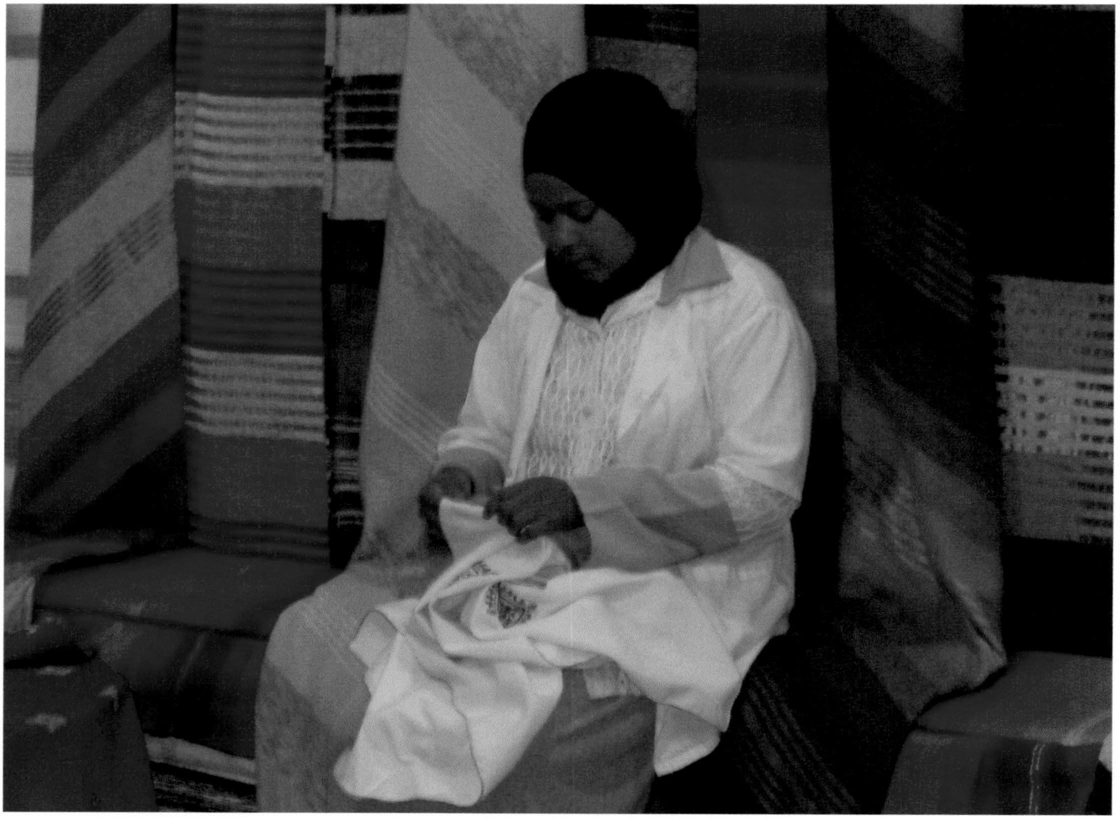

...tablecloths, and the like.

In one area, there is an open circle two meters (6 ft.) in diameter, all three floors above and below, for air… and for yelling (by this I speak of the side of the house, not this quadrangle).

No longer in that rich house, but the sky shows you that we are still south of the Atlas Mountain.

As during our river crossing on the way to Essaouira, only more so do to the mountain.

This town shows you that it was built before the Arabians came with their horses.

The page on the left shows our entrance on to this rocky town from the Southwest. Here we are departing from the East side.

And I am told these rivers are indeed used yearly. "For what, selling used trucks?"

But then again, were the land all dry or all water—irrelevant of thickness—there would be plant life... I think.

Sunday morning had us on the bus by 08:15—this time with our suitcases—to relocate north to city Fes. At 08:40 we stopped to walk through a flea market—a common one, not a tourist soiree.

Continuing north on a route you would call farming territory. Unfortunately, my camera was not thought of at this moment, obviously I need to keep it wrapped around my neck!

This Olive farm on either side shows a half open pipe, 3 feet in diameter, about 4/5 to the brim full of water moving a good 3 mph. Approximately every thousand feet there is another driveway on both sides of this route. There the open pipe becomes covered to dive under the driveway, up on the other side, and then to both travel with the route, and also with the driveways. After a few miles, the pipes are down to eight inches in diameter. After some time, the pipes are slowly enlarging, water from another location.

I saw donkeys and goats drinking at this "canal" that is only two-and-a-half feet high.

At 11:50 AM we entered a town of sixty thousand people, and their main selling is beets. Which reminds me of a story: my mother taking two lads—my brother Bruce and me—to the doctor after we both urinated a red color. The doctor smiled as asking if we had eaten beets. Yes, and it must have been the first time. I see man did not invent the biology of vaccination!

A large number of the cars in this town east of Casablanca are Mercedes-Benz; taxis are smaller than common, and that must be the reason why they all have an open rack on the top, for suitcases (I guess they like to play poker with the rain). All of the buildings and houses are of ochre color, that title given to Marrakech when they call it the "Red City." By 14:00 we were back on the "highway."

An afterthought of olives in Marrakech—this picture was hiding somewhere—and as a rule, olives are not in great need of water, so that canal we drove beside must be for other plants and animals.

This here is right after the olive caucus, though they do muster again, shortly.

By 14:30 we drove past a town that was a small rise in height up the mountain. For 1,600 years it was a Jewish community, with a group of synagogues. As did a number of other hamlets, in 1948 they relocated to Israel; all the synagogues of this town became Mosques.

The city of Meknes is thirty-three miles (53k) west of Fes. The area of these two cities encompasses 160 lakes and reservoirs.

Faces can be deceiving of age. This man here is as quick as a collie.

I made larger copies of this picture, and four other shots, framed and then sent to this restaurant for the boys.
As you see, the river behind the boys, this is all at E L Borj's.

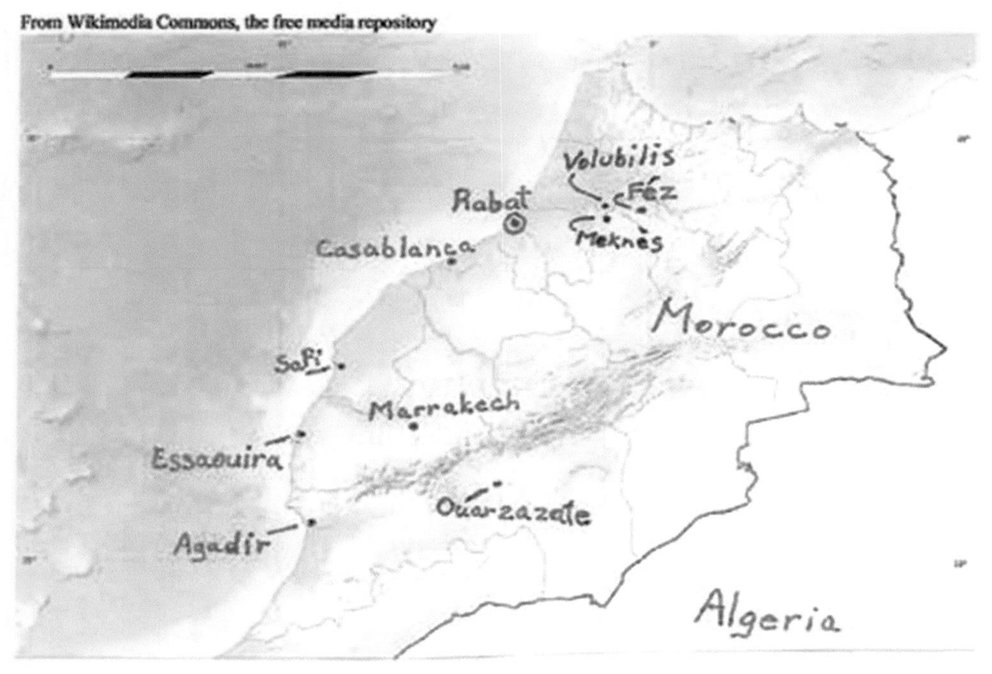

Had we traveled "as the crow flies," the map shows a constant valley route. Half of our way north, we angled further east from which we rose "as the hawk flies." Before arriving at our hotel, we

stopped at a bar, to rejuvenate. The bartender was alone that evening, hence the reason for bringing his wolverine.

Hanging on the rack of this bar were a dozen snow skies. I made a picture of them, but that never came to fruit. There is the power of Ouija that made this picture not ally. To continue to wonder... did this number of people glide down the hill for a few? Are those skies rusty? We shall never know.

After Muhammad died on AD 632, his words spread out in many directions. They arrived to the area of Morocco in AD 680. The Berber people were not so easily swayed. By the year 789, the thousand-year-old city Volubilis became the Capital. Twenty years later, the capital relocated to Fes. As an Islamic leader, a Sultan, died. His title was passed down to his son, that being the name of the dynasty:

Idrisid dynasty	788–974	Fes
Almoravid dynasty	1040–1147	Marrakech
Almohad dynasty	1121–1269	Marrakech
Marinid dynasty	1244–1465	Fes
Idrisid dynasty	1265–1471	Fes
Wattasid dynasty	1471–1554	Fes
Saadi dynasty	1555–1659	Marrakech
Dila'ite Interlude	1659–1663	Fes
Alaouite dynasty	1666–1672	Fes
Alaouite dynasty	1672–1727	Meknes
Alaouite dynasty	1727–1912	Fes
Alaouite dynasty	1912–Present	Rabat

As needed, the old heart of Fes has several thresholds to enter. This is Monday morning. The market we are entering encompasses three hundred thousand people.

Another example of the grinding of marble, and then with liquid to harden it.

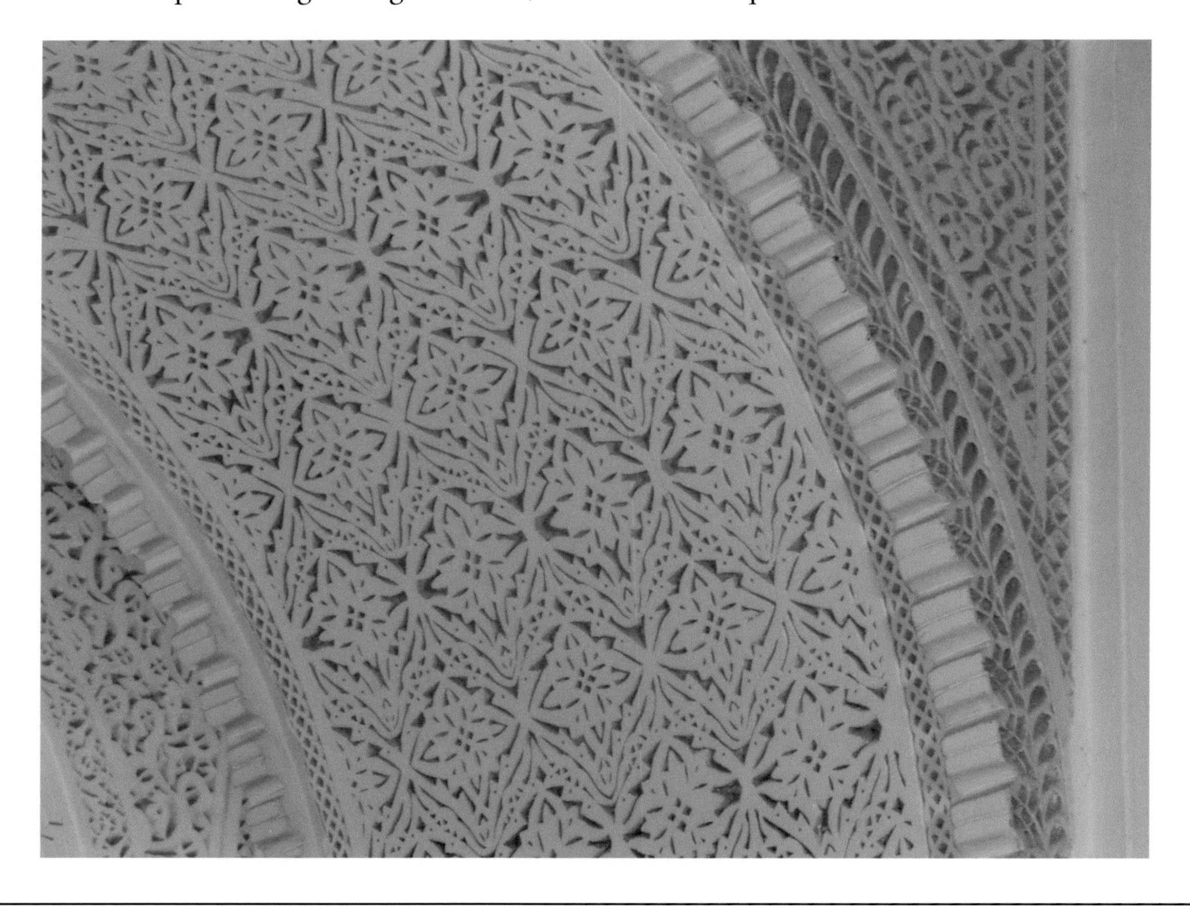

This is only one of 150 Mosques in Fes.

This is the area upon entering our lunch.

Here is the Charnel House of some people whose names I failed to write down.

Could this be an old SINGER?

These monkeys are well trained.

60
160

All of these vases show they were handcrafted intricately.

Our last observation of the fine handcraft being done here in the valley.

Next stop is up the hill...

Is this a fort or a Kasbah? It certainly is larger than an Ouarzazate's Kasbah, vehicles entering.

As all the towns south in the Marrakech state are ochre color, here everywhere, everyone has a deep blue base; maybe they came from Essaouira… kite surfing.

I did not peek in the window, so together we can ponder the need of a 12 ft. wide door, not for a car. Tuesday morning, first stop is at Volubilis.

Volubilis is northwest of the Atlas Mountains, so the constant wind from the Mediterranean makes it quite a usable valley. It became developed by the third century BC under the Carthaginians, though artifacts show people there at 5,000 BC, and those factors are just on the surface.

Carthage is the name of the trading post used by Phoenicia, the country shown below.

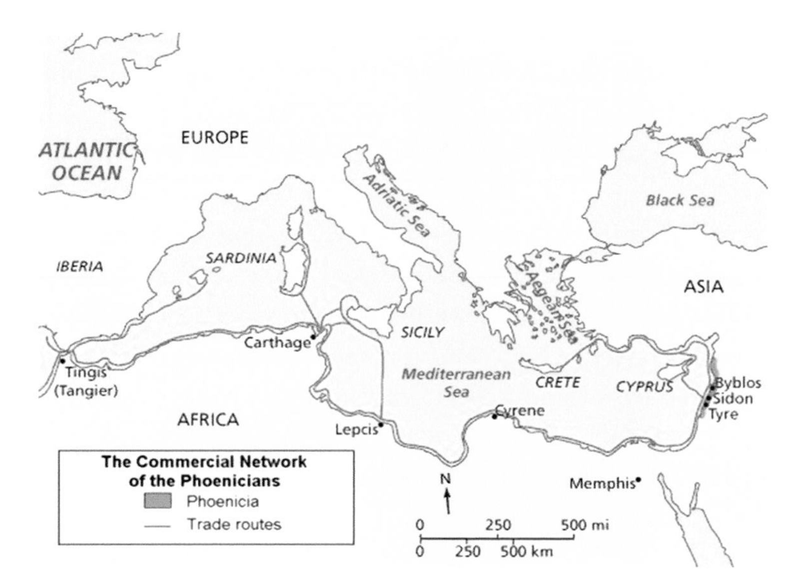

Let us continue our discussion of Volubilis. What was a Phoenician town since 814 BC, became a different town of twenty-thousand Roman citizens. The Basilica you see above, triumphal arch and fine houses with large mosaic floors. The main seller there was olive oil. After some time, it became a requirement to make their town a "gated community." Their area was one hundred acres covered with impressive rocks all around, a 1.6 mile circumference. But after some time, even that was not enough. By AD 285, the Romans did not have their army spread out to its southwest, and they abandoned. It was taken over for seven hundred years, and then with new construction elsewhere, that 1.6 mile of free rock was there for the taking. Then much later in mid-eighteenth century, Volubilis was devastated by an earthquake, and that is when the true looting occurred. It was not until the latter part of the nineteenth century that the site was excavated, revealing many moieties of a two-thousand-year-old city.

Now we can discuss the Phoenicians. The Egyptians arrived just by extending north with the Nile River from their location of birth on the south. But those who settled straight east of the Mediterranean— though we came from the same area of origin—during the colder times when the ice was far past England, ocean liquid was far lower, enough to walk from Ethiopia to Yemen... and then you're off to the races. People needed to live on the type of rivers that have food, clear water, and therefore having the necessary free time for teaching: the east and south sides of China, the west side of India, the two rivers named Tigris and Euphrates that deplete into the Persian Gulf, and of course, the Nile River. Since this is a discussion of the Mediterranean Sea, on the third of those valleys—those rivers in Iraq—we will focus.

Nurture is for not just free time to teach and learn, but more importantly, discover and create, for there is a colder winter in the land as the people enlarged northwest with Tigris and Euphrates, creating the name of the Fertile Crescent. From there they have all learned new tools, so as they curve down to Canaan—the lower part of the east side of the Mediterranean, the drier area— they began tributaries.

The port Byblos must have been perfect for fishing, for upon settling there and making boats from the cedar trees just up the hill of their mountain, they soon became masters of their vessels. This city Byblos is in the country Lebanon, an old name in the Semitic root = "white," in reference to the snowcapped Mount Lebanon. In their spreading out in due time, it was the Byblos fishermen meeting the Egyptians. It was known to be that way, for all the boats for use in Egypt are flat river vessels. That is confirmed by seeing the type of trees that grow in Egypt, they do not have the structure required in making a boat for use in water with big waves.

In "Origin of the Phoenicians," a paper presented by Stanford Holst on June 29, 2008, states, "By 4500 BC the Byblos were in small houses. In 3200 BC, they started making large homes with enclosures as a matter of protection for their now rich artifacts. By 3000 BC, the city (of Byblos) had a massive city wall, with temples, etc." Similar to the steel bone structure used for our high rises, Byblos brought cedar trunks for use in Egypt.

"Buried beside the Great Pyramid in Egypt were two cedar ships, which have been dated to circa 2550 BC. They represent a continuation of the Phoenician cedar trade which began approximately 650 years earlier at Hierakonpolis. Throughout Egypt's long history, its periods of prosperity were marked by the strong evidence of foreign trade, some of which came to its shores borne on Byblos boats." Those Phoenicians brought not just wood, but also olive oil, and wine, from which they received metals and ivory. They became masters in both of those raw materials.

Sidon is a town from 4000 BC, Tyre being a branch south approximately one thousand years later is an island 800m (half 'a mile) from the land.

It was right at that time of 2,750 BC wherein Byblos made agreed rules with cities Sidon and Tyre, in which each became a citystate, a politically independent unit, all having personal laws and religions, and business is competition. In that way, Sidon became the master of silver work and ivory, and glass had only started a few centuries earlier than their invention of glass blowing. There was always rivalry with those works mentioned, and pottery and embroidering and famous metal workers.

This drawing was the best available in Google to show the two enclosed bays of Tyre, one to its north, and one south, that allow ships to dock in heavy wind, with no waves. As you have seen, we are already jumping ahead in time, but all the portraits of Tyre show the dam of this island, and therefore, we must know the reason why this dam was built in 332 BC:

As Alexander of Macedonia was just stepping out to take back their land that was stolen by the Persians almost two hundred years earlier, his first move was to go all the way to Egypt. After having taken Byblos and Sidon, upon arriving at Tyre, he sent some diplomats to allow his army to enter. The heads of his diplomats were thrown over the citadel. It took Alexander from November 333 BC until July 332 BC to complete the dam. The results will not be discussed, but only that all left were sold to slavery.

I spoke previously of the city Byblos and its old settling, not only the oldest settling in Lebanon, but one, maybe the oldest development east of Egypt still in duration, after Baghdad. Baghdad was given the title "city" by it being the first with a garbage dump far away from their living homes. I have read several articles of the history of these old cities in the Mediterranean, and of them all, UNESCO World Heritage Site (United Nations Education, Scientific and Cultural Organization) called Byblos its oldest age at 8,800 BC.

After the bonded connection with Egypt, the Phoenicians continued expanding their travels—no longer just on the coast—and in short order they had not only connected with Cyprus, Crete, entered the Aegean Sea, but in due time all the way around the Mediterranean throughout the third millennium BC. Before this agreement in 2750 BC with Sidon and Tyre, I am sure that Byblos ships entered Cyprus. For all those years as a trader, the Phoenicians spent times of sailing to England to buy tin and stops along the way in Spain.

This is Crete, the big island between Greece and Turkey.

In Crete, they found a very different way of behavior. The people on the large island behaved rather as in an incubator; the only carnivore giving any concern was the otter. And with no heed or apprehension for the arrival of an outside tribe, they never had police, let alone an army. Outside walls or fences were nowhere to be found. And there were some big expensive houses with no gate; everything was open. The physiography of the larger houses was after the years of the arrival of the Phoenicians, but with the continuing lack of the need of police and gates.

Every land has a sport. In Crete it was bull-leaping. It is one thing in Spain to use a red cape as the matador, but quite another to be eye to eye as the bull is arriving, in a position where the bull's horns are low enough for the hands to stable there as the man jumps around, landing on the bull's back, and jumping off, not continuing bareback.

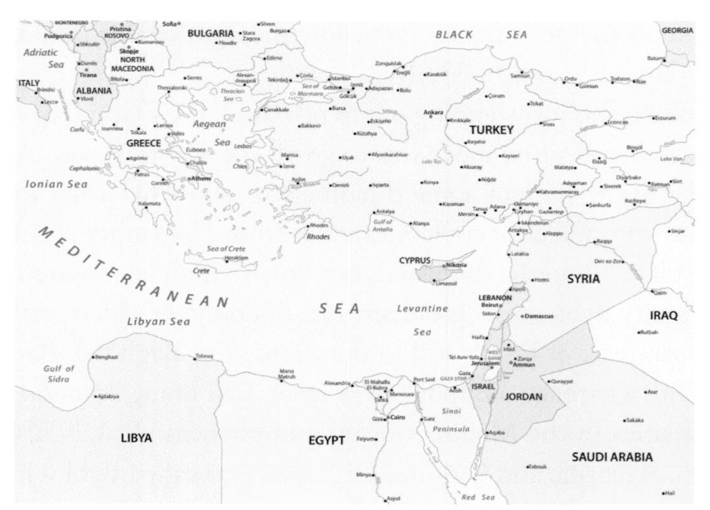

Credit: Rainer Lesniewski

Fossils of humans on Crete have been found dated to 128,000 BC. Though we discussed some Berbery boats docked at Essaouira from time 10,000 BC, this island of Crete is one hundred miles of open water from Greece, and let us not get carried away with the idea of manmade boats of the necessary caliber 130,000 years ago. As we are warming up in the 21st Century, we see the receding of ice from the North Pole, and hence the rising of the ocean's tide. But that is just now. During this Pleistocene Epoch of 2.6 million years, the rhythms of cold temperature versus hot are far greater. It is amid these times of cold when Mother Earth spreads her northern skirt farther south, thus giving a hand for the northern Asians to go further east, or the French to enter England, and those of the warmer climate to walk through shallow parts of the sea.

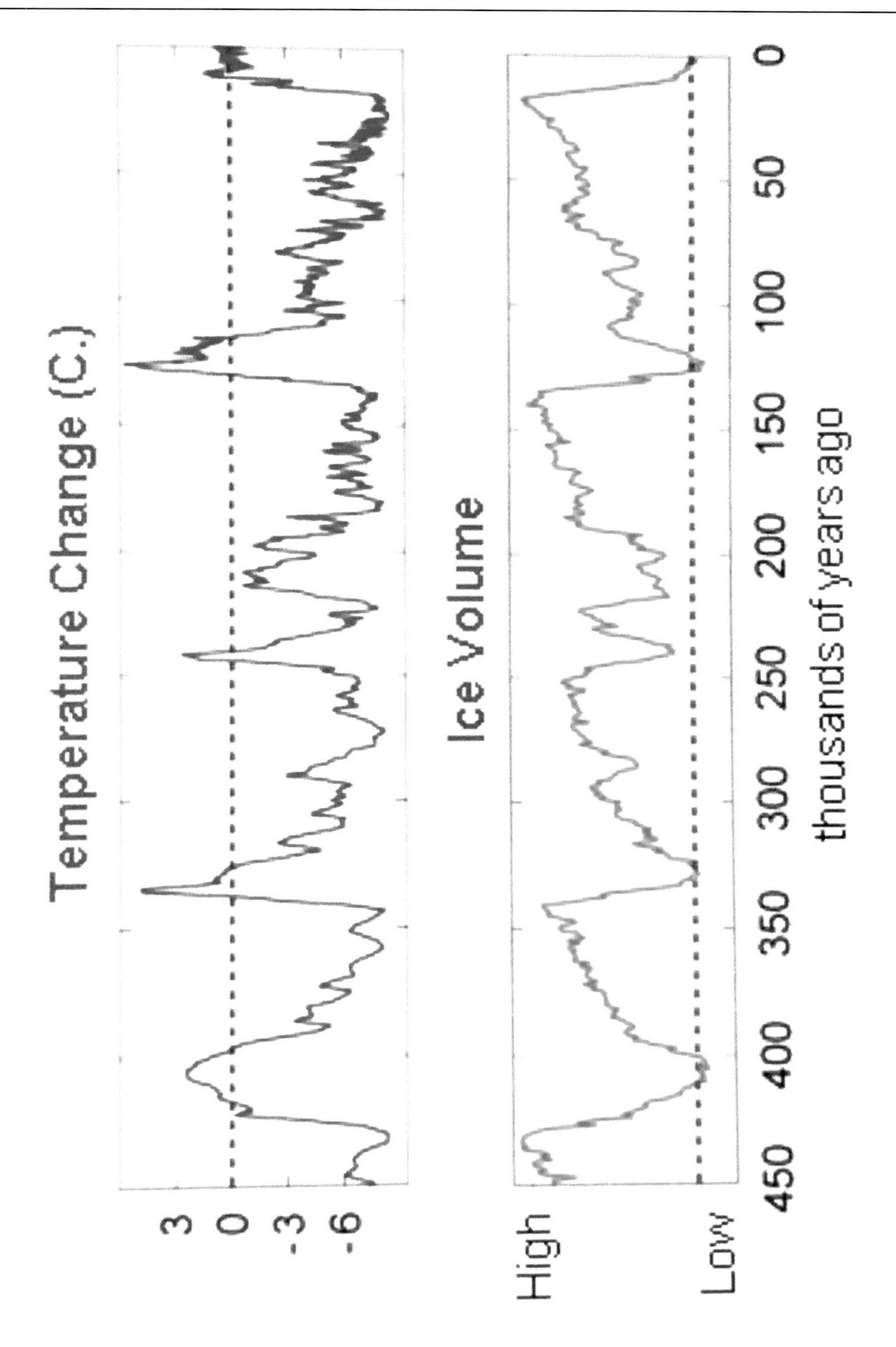

Graph of Temperature Change and Ice Volume. Produced by Dennis O'Neil (based on a graph entitled Ice Age Temperature Changes produced by Robert A. Rohde, University of California, Berkeley)

This map is rather an X-ray through the water, showing a ring of Greece, Crete, and Turkey, with the Aegean Sea as a plate, not a bowl.

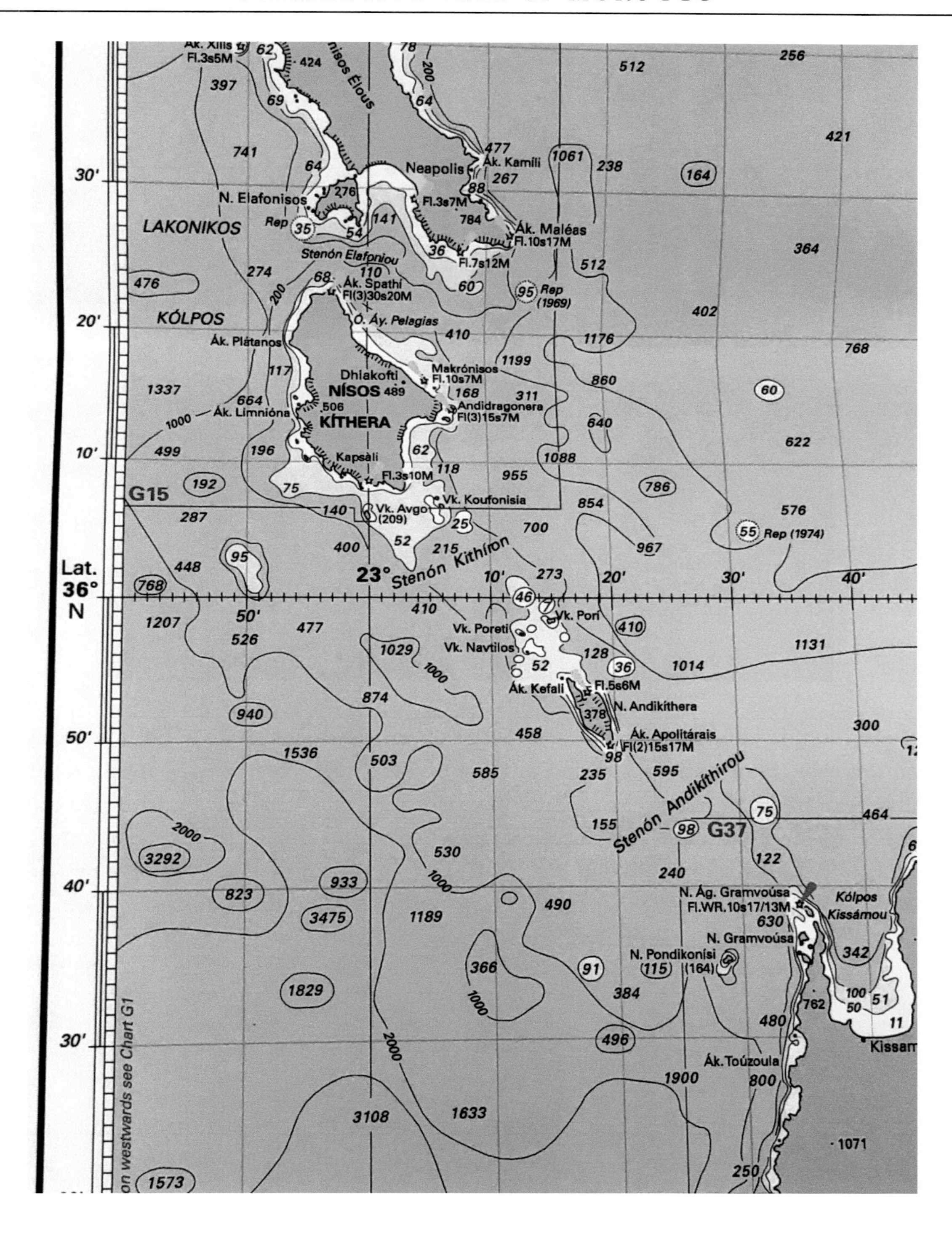

This chart by Imray shows the walking path from Greece onto Crete at 20,000 BC; 140,000 BC; 250,000 BC; 345,000 BC...all the way to the beginning of the Pleistocene, 2.6 million years ago. In 1971 a human fossil was found in Sale, Morocco, dated 400,000 BC, so any of those "winter times" mentioned above will do.

As the Phoenicians mingled with the Minoans, they were of the same "Bonobo" DNA, both became traders, and Minoan made their title of city-state a mere fifty years later, at 2,700 BC. But they were not protégé to Phoenicia; the Minoans already had vessels with two masts for sailing. Minoan started trading on their route to Egypt, Canaan, Cyprus, the Levantine coasts, Anatolia, and the Greek mainland. Of the many items that the Minoans sold: wood, wine, olive oil, wool, cloth, herbs, and most impressively, purple dye, but not until 1,750 BC.

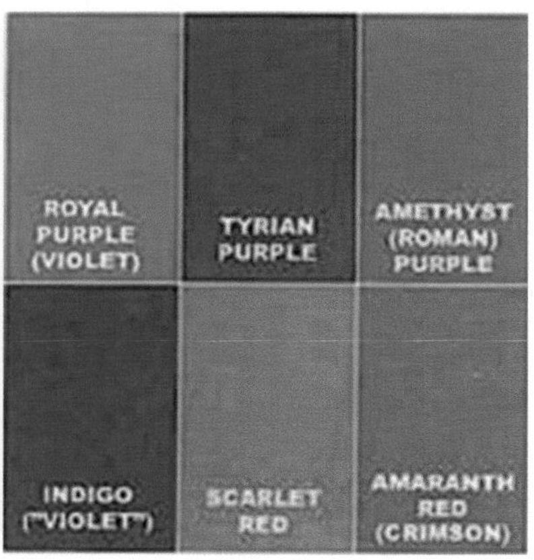

This dye was not just simply seeing the small secretion within these sea snails, but the use of its "ink" on clothing, the new enrapturing colors that only deepen with age, as compared to the regular dye of jeans, or other wall paint. The sunlight actually brightens the dye. David Jacoby remarked that "twelve thousand snails of Murex brandaris yields no more than 1.4g of pure dye, enough to color only the trim of a single garment." Murex shellfish was apparently first seen in the Aegean Sea—the bay between Greece and Turkey—the main reason being that the depth there is not so far down, as can be confirmed by the number of islands in the area. Tyrian purple was the most expensive.

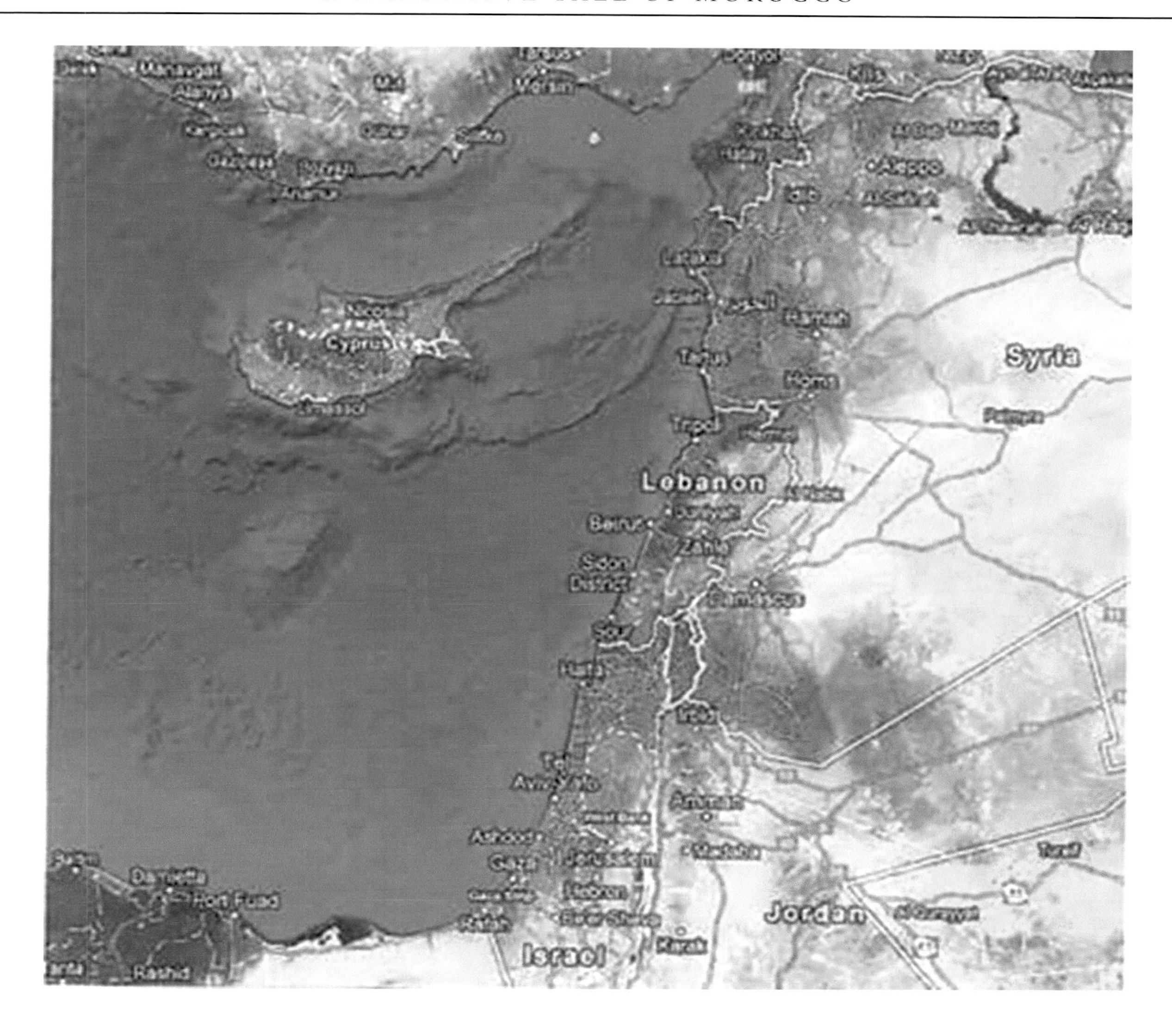

Cyprus

Though I have seen no displays of fossils found on Cyprus earlier than 8500 BC, I do not believe that people entered onto Crete before they were on Cyprus. On this map, can you not see yourself holding your boots in your hand as you walk out from Syria? So henceforth, that's my call: as early as the entering onto Crete were people entering onto Cyprus. Approximately 3,000 BC was the time of not looking for, but finding vast amounts of Copper. They refined their copper, and for 2,500 years, all sailed to Cyprus to buy copper. That is how they got so rich: no requirement of army, no ships for trading—"bring the mountain to the man." As we have many Greek names, so is Cyprus = Greek for Copper.

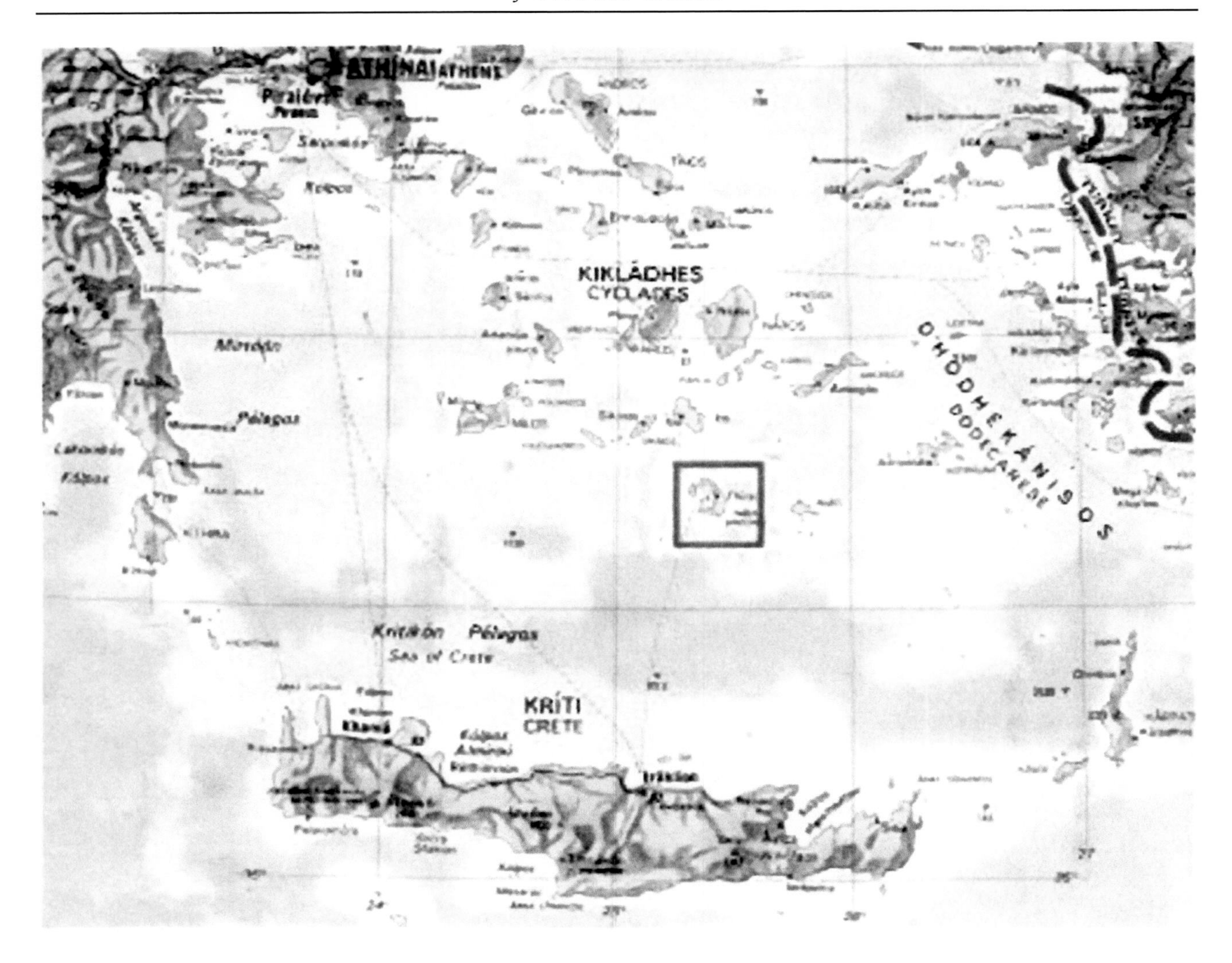

The Red square on this map is the island Thera.

In Wikipedia: Minoan eruption. "The Minoan eruption of Thera, also referred to as the Thera eruption, was a major catastrophic volcanic eruption with a Volcanic Explosivity Index of 6 or 7 and a dense-rock equivalent of 60 km3. The eruption was one of the largest volcanic events on Earth in record history. The eruption devastated the island of Thera (also called Santorini), including the Minoan settlement named Akrotiri, as well as communities and agricultural areas on nearby islands and on the coast of Crete. Another method used to establish the date of eruption is tree-ring dating. Tree-ring data has shown that a large event interfering with the normal tree growth in North America occurred during 1629–1628 BC. Evidence of a climatic event around 1628 BC has been found in studies of growth depression of European oaks in Ireland and of Scotch pines in Sweden. Bristlecone pine frost rings also indicate a date of 1627 BC."

Akrotiri

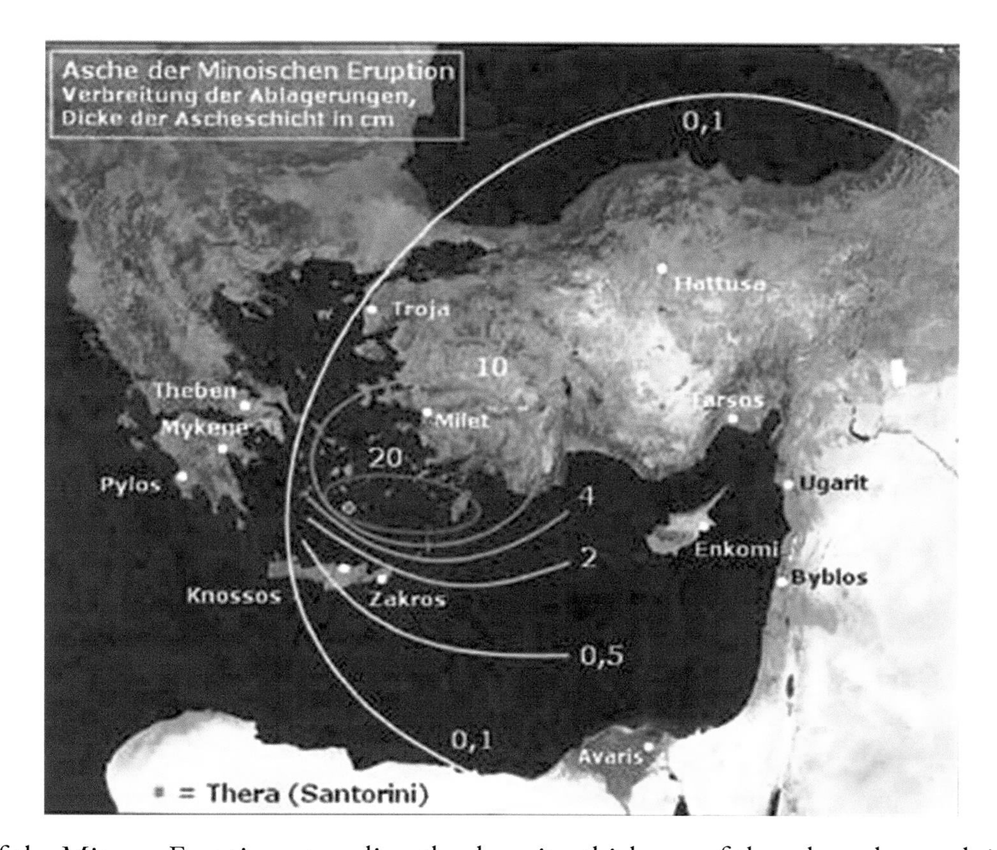

Ashes of the Minoan Eruption, spreading the deposits, thickness of the ash to the south is intense

The Minoan's colony of Akrotiri, Thera, might have had a quick, painless death; we know not. All the puff of the Thera dragon burst straight up five miles high, hence the reason for the wide, waterless cloud that took a year to open the sun to the Northern hemisphere, as shown by those trees.

Wikipedia

On 1,630 BC, Thera was one island.

Thera

The north side of Crete received a lot of ash. All the farms on Crete's east side became unusable, and that alone has me conclude that some amount of the Minoans relocated to Phoenicia. Further ahead in time of both history and the pages of this journal, you will learn of the opening up of some part of Cretan land of its north/ east that was covered up on 1629 BC, so deeply so, that the land was only found while doing construction of buildings above it 3,527 years later in AD 1898. The Minoans and Phoenicians were friends together for a thousand years before the Thera eruption, and by the larger houses after the Phoenicians arrived at Minoan, one can make a betting assumption that some number of Phoenicians lived on Crete.

In the same way that in AD 2013, Brazil paid for six thousand Cuban Doctors to arrive and work in rural areas, Phoenicians that lived in Crete allowed Minoans to live with them, for the benefit of both.

Piraeus, Greece, has been inhabited historically since the 26th Century BC. This statement of inhabitation is only a record of art and painting, for it is a great fishing area, hence, far older. The location is simply the bay of the river depleting from Athens, but it was strictly a place to dock their fishing boat, for the water is very deep, the rocky land of the bay almost a wall. The Mediterranean is a large branch of the Atlantic Ocean, but having such a small canal at its western end gives the Mediterranean no high tide–low tide as compared to the Bay of Fundy on the other side of the Atlantic, a whiplash of high tide–low tide of forty feet. Those high rocks in Piraeus of which I spoke are perfect for that time every year when the dry season has the Mediterranean dropping low enough for the scraping off of salt from the wall. That is all Greece was then, fishermen for another five hundred years. Mycenae is the name of a city as old as Piraeus, and as the area developed in stature and size, Mycenaean became the name to discuss, the name of over half of Greece on the south side, the name of the maker of the Trojan horse. We cannot speak of the moment wherein the Mycenaeans investigated Crete, for they are only one hundred miles north of Crete, and therefore, not unscathed by the Thera eruption. They themselves had cleanup work to do before checking out their Cretan neighbor.

This eruption of island Thera was more than a five-mile high explosion, but also a tsunami wave that brought unusual fish to the streets. When looking in Google for pottery and vase from the streets of Crete, as the group of centuries are placed, those from the Minoan - Mycenaean time of 1,600 - 1,200 BC are far more intricate, and not all, but most have an octopus on their symbol; one of the items from the bed of the sea, and no doubt, something they had never seen.

'The Time Machine' and 'The Twilight Zone,' to name a few, did not invent Extraterrestrial!

The Mycenaeans pretty much owned Crete after the Thera Eruption for over 400 years, until the arrival of the 'Sea People' in 1,200 BC. The vases and potteries found by Arthur Evans were covered up for 3,528 years, and therefore, more precisely calculate their age. The centuries of covered vases are more precise than the claimes of the governless "Viking" type.

The Phoenicians are known to have become a monopoly of murex dye. But we know how that became so. Had there been no Thera Eruption, then there is no way to believe in the Phoenicians having even half of the market– the Minoans being the "inventor and master" of the dye, the "inventor" of two sail masts, and just as smooth on the sea as they trade from port to port for a thousand years together with the Phoenicians.

During the time of approximately 1500 BC, Egypt paid for Phoenician Captains to make maps of his way south down both the Atlantic and Arabian Sea.

There is a name of people called "the Sea People", from the land just north of the Mycenaean Greeks, who are described as "a confederacy of seafaring raiders," showing that the Vikings did not invent invading by water. And as the Vikings did settle on two of their raided spots, Dublin and York, so did the Sea People settle in Crete between 1,200 and 1,000 BC. They also settled in their traveling of the Aegean Sea all the way to spots in the south/west part of now Turkey. There are some writers that not only give the Sea People a more specific location of birth in Greece, but also a different name, that being the Dorians—a small district in the center of Greece called Doris, just north of the Mycenaean. Since their time is before the Dark Age, all the historian statements are vague, they being not makers, but takers, so no artifacts to show their time. We piece between real and mythical stories, and history by Homer.

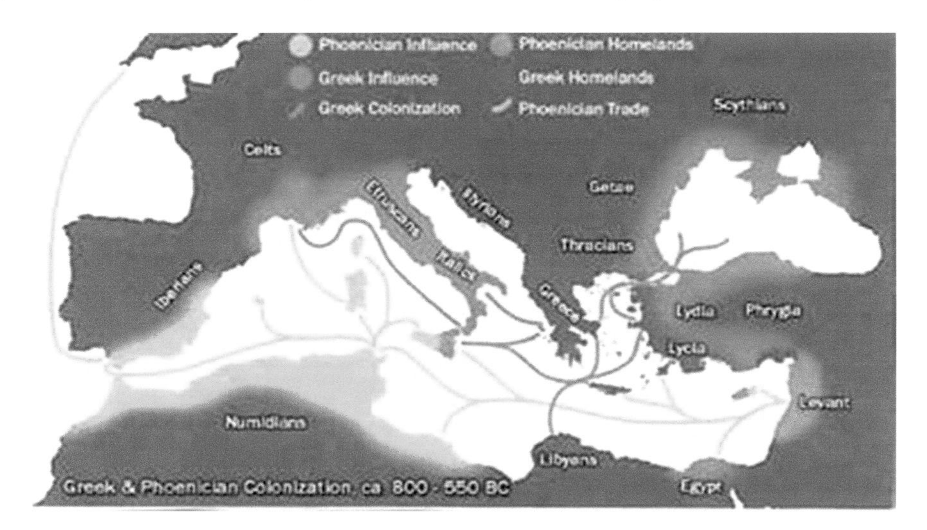

In 814 BC, Carthage, Tunisia was the first land in which they left some Phoenicians there. The Phoenicians settled in Crete almost two thousand years earlier, but there, in settled ports. There were I am sure several other ports wherein Phoenicians settled; helping business. Carthage was not a port, just vertical rock, a fort for making salt, and that must be why it was given that title of new, for settling open land. As the years went forward, Carthage became a city of renown, a trader of large asset. There came to be over two hundred trading posts in the Mediterranean and the Black Sea, and it became almost as Carthage defended the West, and Tyre defended the East; though both free trading within each other's area, as it was with the Minoans. As a rule, when trading with the Berbers as early as 2000 BC, the Phoenicians would pay commissions up-front for the year, and then upon arriving at any agreed port, the freight was there for the pick-up. Clever. In 1000 BC, the Capital of Phoenicia was relocated from Byblos to Tyre.

After the 1000 BC–800 BC Dark Age of Greece, as cities developed wishing to become in a structure way, they were specific in their type of government from city to city. For the first new century, 800 to 700 BC, some cities were no less tyrant than the Dorians. Athens, not one of them, became the focus of the adult structure. Some parts of Greece became sailors out of need of food, and also for much rebirth of tyranny. In 750 BC Greece began a 250 years of expansion, settling colonies in all directions.

As Greece began to develop, spreading throughout the northern Mediterranean—no longer called Mycenaean—the Greeks were of Colonization, as compared to Phoenicia and Minoan being strictly Traders. As Greece enlarged south of Italy, they saw a fleet of Phoenician/Carthage ships in Sicily. The Greeks were given the east side of Sicily. To the Greeks, the Phoenicians gave not only a piece of the pie, but guidance for traveling at night via the North Pole. We all know that Greece gave us Pi x r. But those actual numbers come from Phoenicia, with the circle of 360 degrees. We have very little record of journalistic presentations by the Phoenicians; for all we know, such Greek displays are copies of Phoenician work.

Of all the things that the Phoenicians gave us, the most impressive is their invention of letters. Until that time, though numbers were basic, writing was the use of symbols that were not well known, total control of transaction. Similar to secretary shorthand, or more so than that, shorthand typewriting used during trial with the use of a smaller number of syllables/symbols, needing to be the speed of a tape recorder. Letters by the Phoenicians were the Internet of their time. It was started at 1300 BC to 800 BC Phoenicia's peak, with all business written by letter, and why all the western languages—Russia an extension from the west—use letters.

After their time of being able to live without the Sea People, the Greeks connected with the idea of letters in 800 BC. Had there been no Confederacy by the Dorians, it would have been four hundred years earlier. Greece enjoyed the letters so much that they added vowels. The Phoenicians as said are an extension from Iraq, where symbols started by hammer and chisel, hence from right to left. With the invention of ink in 2,500 BC in Egypt and China, the Phoenicians continued their direction of symbols while writing with letters, from right to left. In 700BC Greece soon changed their direction of writing to be from left to right, and that domino went through Latin, all European and Russian languages writing from left to right. As mentioned earlier, Lebanon is the name of their land since they first arrived. Their nickname is under the Greek word: phoinos = "blood red," in reference to Tyrian purple, the most expensive. But they made and sold all the colors from the sea snail mollusks all over the Mediterranean, the Black Sea, and islands outside of Essaouira, Morocco. Monopoly from 1,550 BC until 332 BC.

The Jewish loved the idea of writing by letters even more than anyone; for now all their stories of their religion can be on "paper," no longer need everything memorized, all the stories spoken, the ability to read, to spread their knowledge. To show their gratefulness, the name of the inventor: Byblos. In English, Bible.

Beginning in the eighth Century BC, the Phoenicians made ships to suit the work at hand. They invented the "bireme" vessel, oars placing on different decks.

This bireme shown here is one for use in action: the mast is removable, the keel from the stern is close to that of the stem, allowing one to reverse after neutralizing the opponent. I imagine this would be the perfect vessel to accompany a group of ships as they travel from port to port, of course, mast up. This shepherd of the flock is as nimble as the man we saw in Morocco.

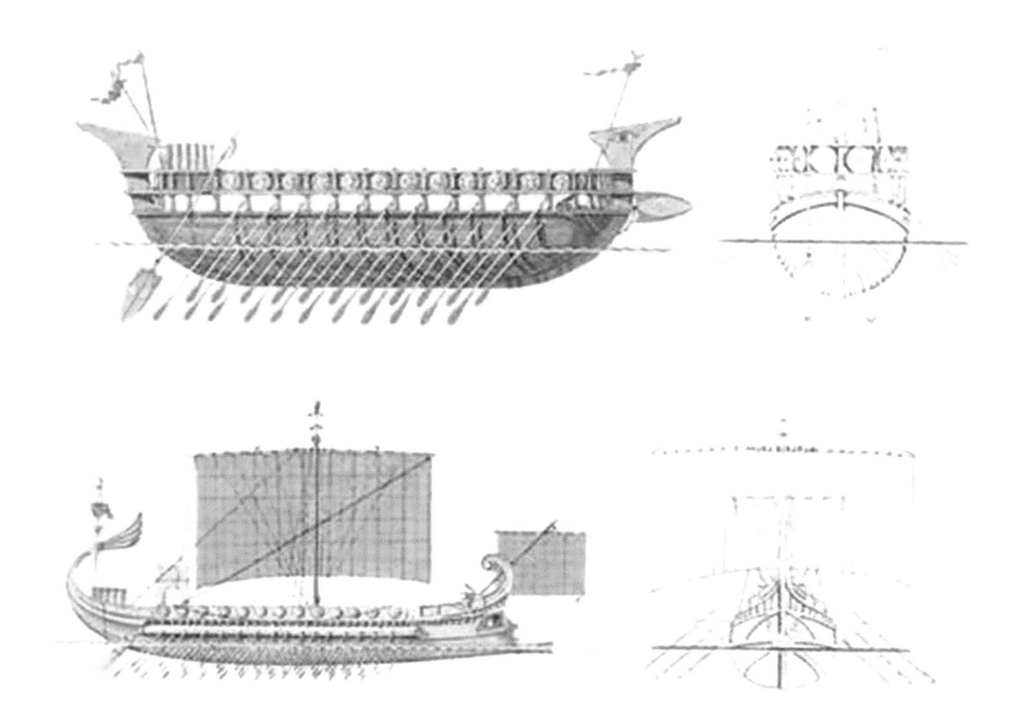

The trireme above is one for action as well. With no ballast, she displaces only forty tons (36,364 K). "Triremes of this type are said to have been capable of reaching speeds greater than seven knots (8 miles per hour) and perhaps as high as nine knots under oars." -Wikipedia

For the record: a mile = 5,280 feet; a nautical mile = 6,076 feet [Random House: 'Fathom' 1) a nautical unit of length equal to 6 feet. 2) to measure the depth of water by a sounding line] - a very old Radar. Probably, a nautical mile was 6,000 feet, but no doubt in the 20th Century tuned it to 6,076 feet to make the Earth 24,000 nautical miles of circumference at the equator; Captains of the sea and Pilots of the air always use nautical maps.

"Further down the last millennium of BC, it is written that of all the lands who had slavery, Greece had the greatest number of slaves per free, 20 to 1, than anyone" (Wikipedia). And yet, in his Republic, "Plato contends that the love of money is a tendency of the soul found amongst Phoenicians and Egyptians, which distinguishes them from the Greeks who tend toward the love of knowledge." In his laws, he asserts "that this love of money has led the Phoenicians and Egyptians to develop skills in cunning and trickery rather than wisdom." Some of Greeks' slaves were bought from the Phoenicians—my idol!

At this moment, we are now moving ahead to AD 1890 and at Crete.

Arthur Evans was a British archaeologist, as was his father, John Evans. They both received the title "Sir" after doing unique and useful work for the benefit of all. John Evans's work was all done in England. He was the first to devise a systematic classification of British Iron Age, among a great number of other meticulous collecting of artifacts. Arthur Evans continued the help on the island, but his "Sir" comes from work done abroad. He had found some amulets (a charm worn to ward off evil) in Crete, and then all his holidays from 1894–1899 had Evans back there, delving throughout Crete. He was looking for prealphabetic writing. Evans found items of art and building structure that was far advanced for their time.

The city Iraklio is on the land north-center of Crete, just in from the sea. A construction of a building there revealed an extensive site. This extensive site in Irakio gives a confirmation of that claim of waves of 150 feet in height and the covering up of Knossos. At about that same time, Britain and France told Ottoman to leave Crete on 1898.

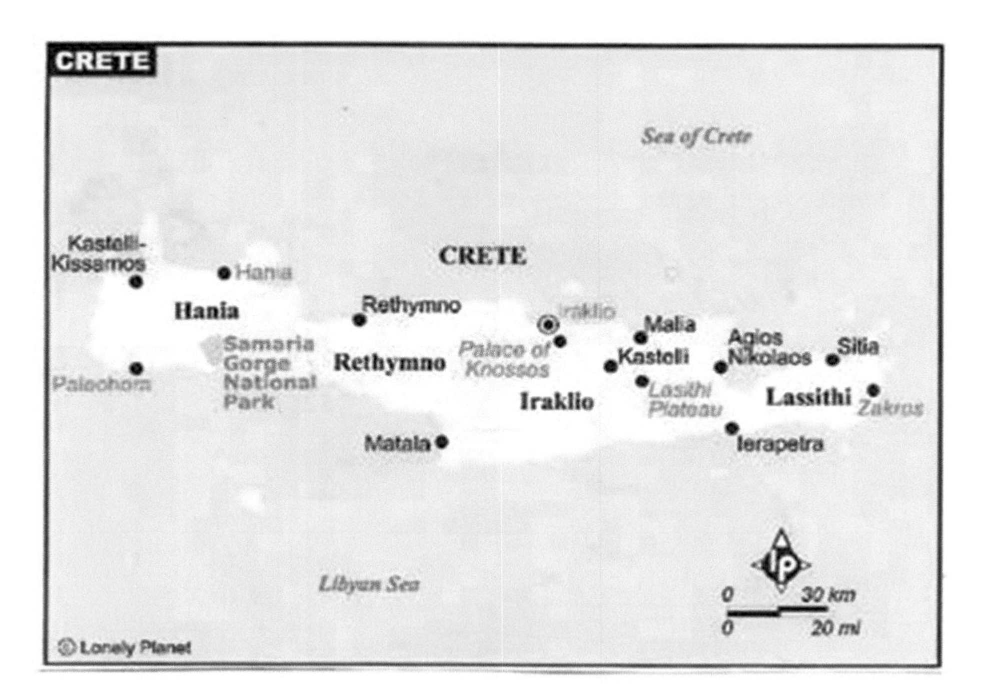

Evans was able to purchase the whole site and begin his excavating In five seasons from 1900 to 1905 he laid bare the full enermous palace.

"Evans was able to purchase the whole site and begin his excavating. In five seasons from 1900 to 1905 he laid bare the full enormous palace. There were several later seasons on the periphery, but he then spent the rest of his life writing a report on his excavations in four massive volumes and at the same time building up the whole history of what he named the Minoan Civilization, assigning it to 3 phases: the Early Minoan (EM), the Middle Minoan (MM), and the Late Minoan (LM)" (http://www.civilization.org.uk/minoans/sir-arthur.evans):

Arthur Evans Theodore Fyfe Ducan Mackenzie

Theodore Fyfe, Christian Doll, and Piet de Jong were all professional, highly skilled architects with their accurate, measured plans and elevations of a very large, long lived, and exceptionally complex palace site.

Ducan Mackenzie was an excellent field archaeologist, carefully recorder of walls, stratigraphy, and other finds, with a flair for Minoan ceramics.

In Greek mythology, Minos was one of Zeus's sons, and he became King of Crete, so Evans changed the name of discussion in history to be Minoan. But what came first, King Minos of Crete, who ruled around the time of 1350–1250 BC, or Zeus's son Minos?

Kamarais pottery (c.2000 BC) and brilliant frescoes from a palace were exposed. The fact that they were covered up since 1629 BC is shown by the perfect, no fossil breakdown.

It is difficult to say who invented the idea of pottery wheels. Egypt; Mesopotamia; Crete (Minoan); Tokyo. In Japan, pots are shown dated to 14,000 BC, but just pottery; the name of wheels was not mentioned. The idea of 'wheels' in use in making a vase: the center of the vase is placed on the center of a circular plate that can turn by use of the feet, at a good enough speed to make smooth, perfect vases, allowing all the work to be done far better, and all by one person. Clay is dark and painted with white and red. Depict figures of the nature world waves and fishes.

Minoan Bull-leaper

From Wikipedia: "The Minoan bull-leaper is a bronze group of a bull and leaper in the British Museum. It is the only known largely complete three-dimensional sculpture depicting Minoan bull-leaping. Although bull-leaping certainly took place in Crete at this time, the leap depicted is practically impossible, and it has therefore been speculated that the sculpture may be an exaggerated depiction. This spectacular has been backed up the testaments of modern day bull-leaping in France and Spain."

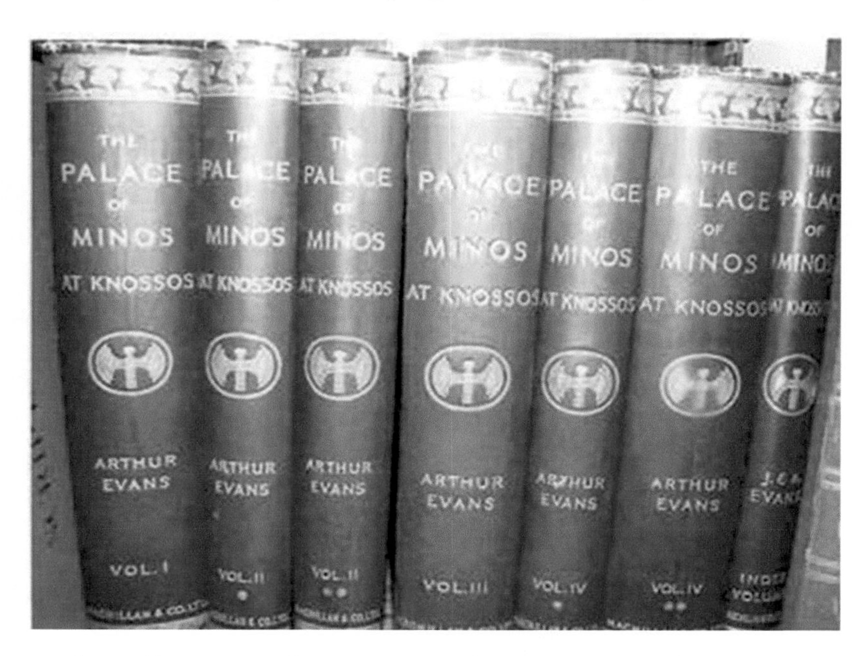

http: // www. civilization. Org.uk/minoan/sir-arthur evans

Arthur Evans, the excavator of Knossos, first published this object in the Journal of *Hellenic Studies.* Evans dated the bull-leaper to the Late Minoan I period, so that this object dates to approximately 1600 BC.

It was acquired by the British Museum in 1966 as part of the collection of Captain Edward George Spencer-Churchill (1876-1964). He acquired it in Crete in 1921. The object was widely known before its acquisition and display in the Museum. It was illustrated in several general books and exhibited at the British Academy in 1936.

Bull-leaping

"Bull-leaping and bulls in general are believed to have been an important part of Minoan culture. Excavations at Knossos have revealed several frescos depicting bull-leaping. It has been suggested bulls may have had some religious significance to them. For example: the large, exaggerated size of the bull compared to the human leaper may give an idea of the Minoans' reverence for the power of the animal." [1] – (Not considered though, is the size of people in general, those 2,000 BC)

Arthur Evans, the excavator of Knossos, first published this object in the Journal of Hellenic Studies. Evans dated the bull-leaper to the Late Minoan I period, so that this object dates to approximately 1600 BC.

The Minoan bull leaper from the front

This object has been central to discussions of bull-leaping, since Arthur Evans used it as the basis for his reconstruction of the mechanics of the leap: the leaper grabs the bull's horns, executes a back flip onto the bull's back and then dismounts.[5] As John Younger has pointed out, although this reconstruction has become part of bull-leaping in the popular imagination, comparatively few Minoan depictions show exactly this schema. The majority show the leaper diving over the bull's horns onto the back.

Not only were half of the priests in Minoan female, but here is the "Snake Goddess" performing a ritual.

Of the two languages at Minoan, this is the older, Linear A as of yet undeciphered.

Linear B was from the arrival of the Greek-Mycenaeans. It was deciphered by Michael Vintrio and John Chadwick in the 1950's.

The Minoan's colony of Akrotiri, Thera, might have had a quick, painless death; we know not. All the puff of the Thera dragon burst straight up 5 miles high, hence the reason for the wide waterless cloud that took a year to open the sun to the northern hemisphere, as shown by the trees. And also the reason why Evans did not at first see the maker of the amulets; Knossos was covered up, as displayed on page 81. Much of the construction was gone, but the bone structure was not decimated, and Fyfe, Doll, Jong and Mackenzie were able to rebuild the palace. The intention of the construction was to fabricate then mold the public castle just the point of knowing its size, and ability to walk inside and see some fixed-up art within.

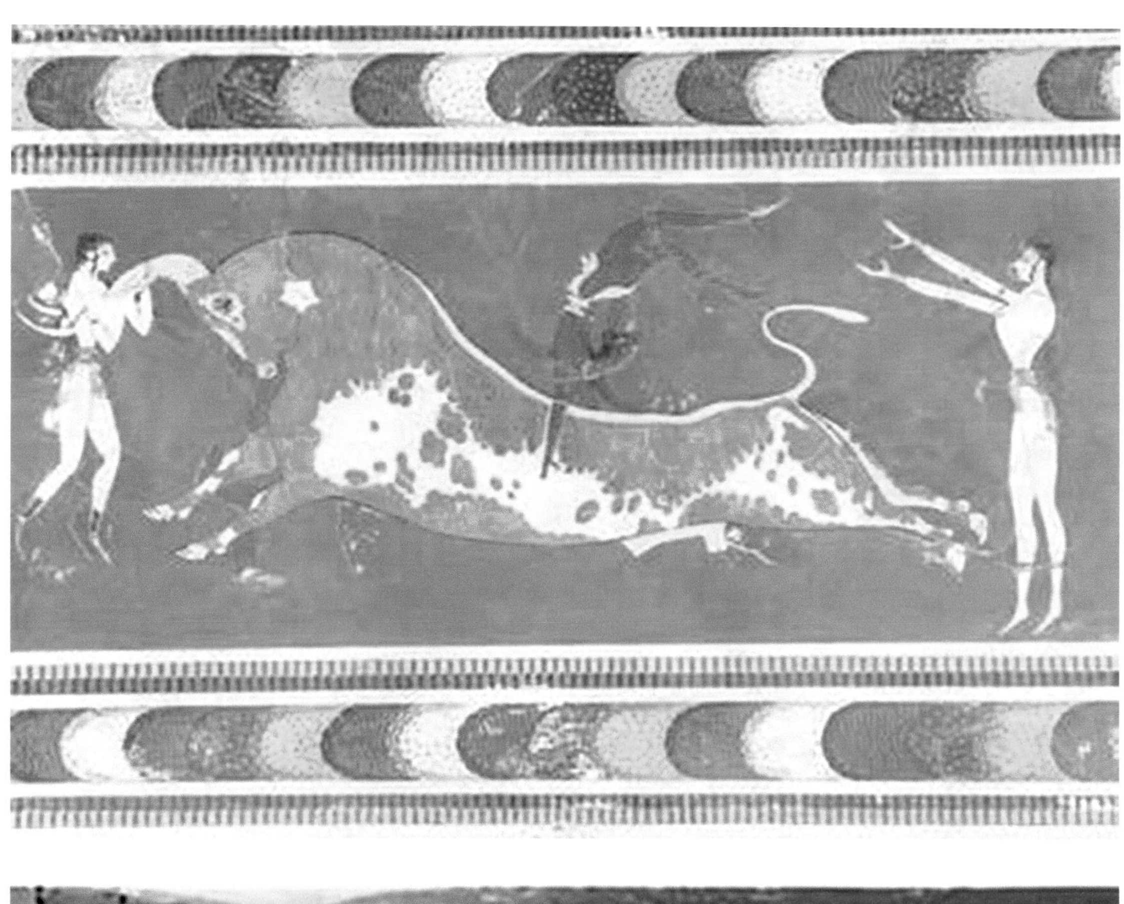

Anywhere dolphins are seen, they are enjoyed through time immortal.

Minoan Bull-leaper
From Wikipedia, the free encyclopedia

Here are the present jumpers in France and Spain that were mentioned on page 88.

The 'red cape' in use here keeps the bulls' head low.

This picture of Thera is quite recent, with the smaller version of eruption being on 1956; another on 1950. But it is such a perfect area that the tourists return; just like Agadir, Morocco.

Now we sail west back to Morroco, though continuing in history.

We spoke earlier of the boats used in Essaouira, 10,000 BC. They are the Berber people. Their name is used not only in reference to people in the North - West of Africa's history, but right up to now, as their unique language is one of three in Morocco: French; Arabic; Berber. This is similar to certain islands in the West Indies and Louisiana, where Creole is usable with the government.

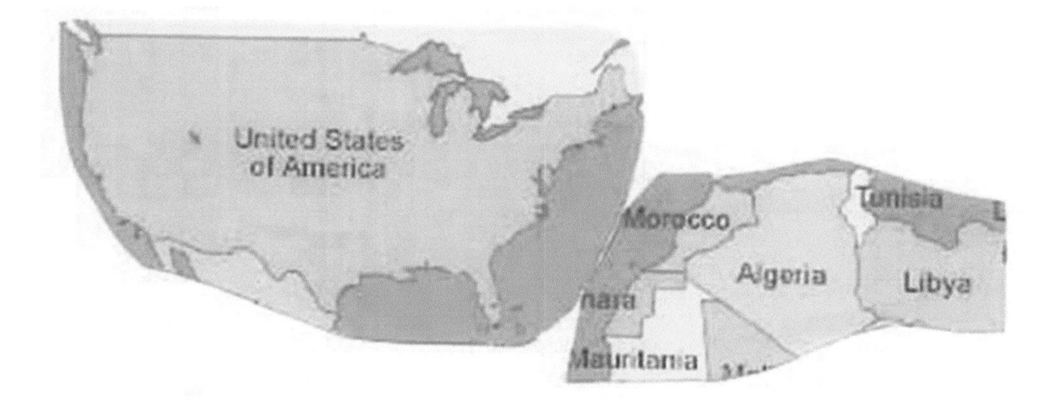

20,000 B.C. was not just colder, with low tide on the ocean, but Sahara was not a desert. Fossil of plants at that time in Sahara were those in need of more water to stay alive. An easy time for people to disperse west of Egypt when the ground has edible plants throughout. The area that you see here, was all Berber land. It became so during the times when the warmth made Sahara more and more desertish, and therefore, people roaming for food, contacting with others, and hence the reason why this whole area – over half the size of U.S. – was all one language; you know they were roaming with a purpose.

A moor is a child of a Berber and an Arab. It was the Moors who rose north from Morroco to conquer Spain. Portugal and south France in AD 711.

By A.D. 1,150, Portugal had half of their land back; A.D. 1.166 all returned by Geraldo Geraldes, Sempavor "without fear". It took until A.D. 1492 - "The Fall of Grenada" - to end Muslim in Iberia (Portugal & Spain). We all have a couple of 'Alexanders'.

It is impressive the number of centuries the Moors held the Iberia.

Here is Geraldes holding the cut head of a Moor. Geraldes used tactical maneuvers of climbing the Kasbah late at night and doing all their killing by surprise; or entering the area day time during the rain; etc. Portugal was whole, a good 200 years before "The Fall of Granada" and the very bottom of Spain, end of Moors. Still, that is only traveled north, for there continued whatever amount at home in Morocco. The Berbers may have diminished their number in their land, but that only demonstrates their ability to adapt, and stay on top. And I say their name, not Moor, to claim their difference. The idea of piracy was not new, but it became a venture for the Berbers in 1471 AD and the founding of town Chefchaouen, in Riff.

Their piracy grew in its daring, its strength, and its size, no longer in just Chefchaouen, but also Junis, Algiar, Tangier and Tripoli. By the 16th century into the 19th century, they no longer just stole goods, but people; for ransom if they are rich, or for sale to the slavetrade during those 300 years, 800,000 to 1.25 million people were enslaved by the Barbaries.

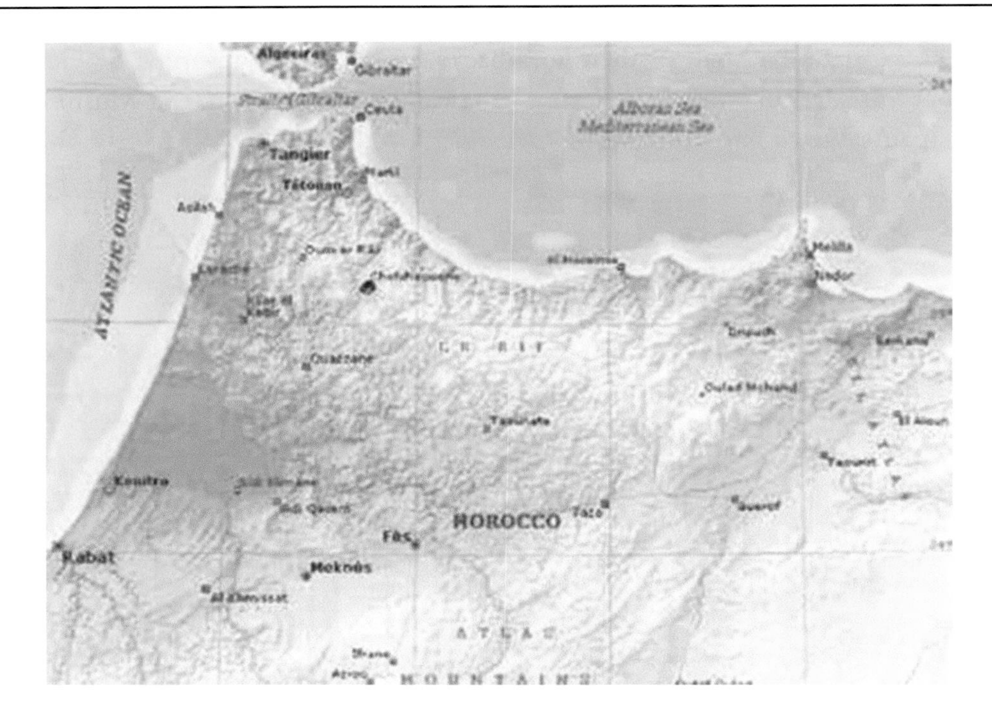

Chefchaouen, Morocco

The Riff Mountains are as seen on the south-west of the Mediterranean. – right up to the sea, making a great number of rivers for boats to say, "come and get me."

The only difference between these pirates and those of recent time from Somalia is an engine and bigger guns.

Corsairs – a pirate vessel, especially formerly of Barbary,
a region of N. African Random House Dict.

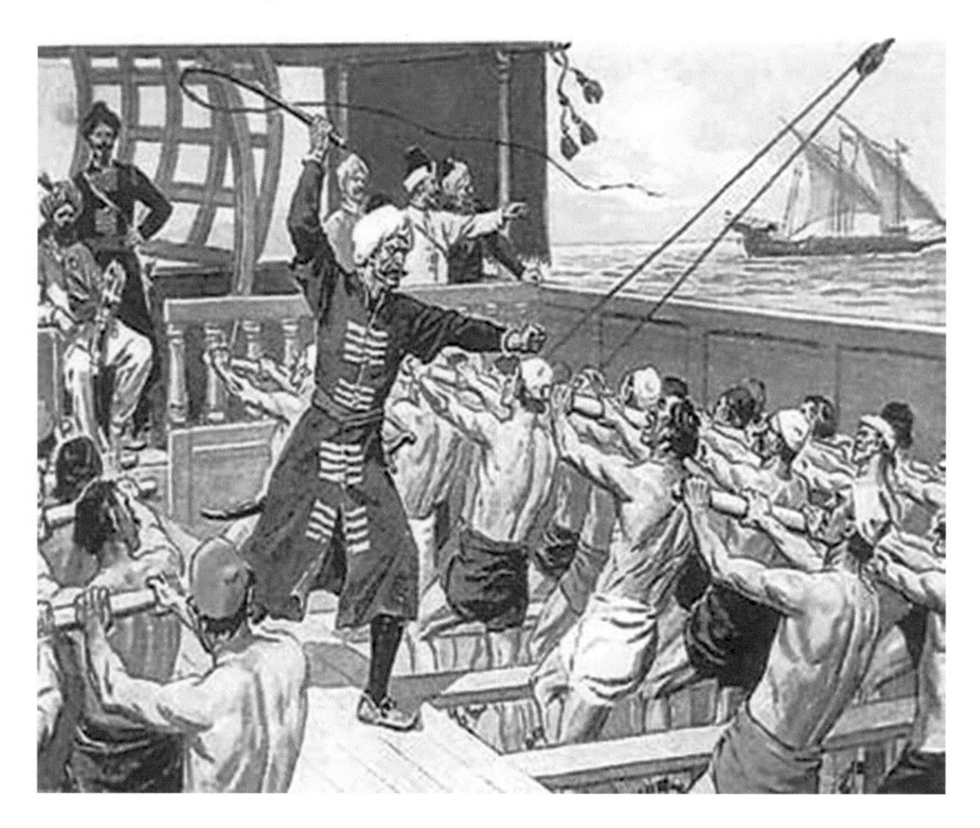

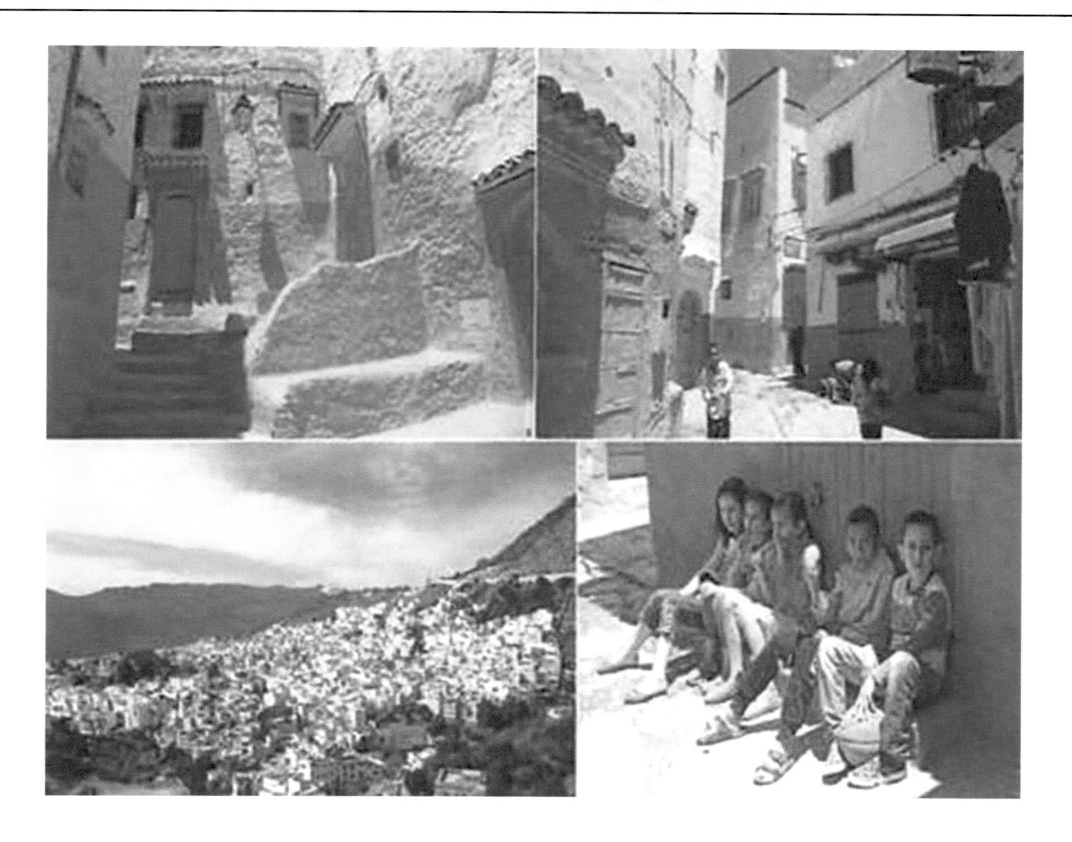

These Wikipedia shots of Chefchaouen show that this town is even more bluer than Fes.

This page is still in Chefchaouen.

Showing the time of Egypt's strength is the 1,500 BC year when Phoenicia began to trade at Asilah (above). Not beeing told the years, but no doubt now is when Egypt paid for mapping of Africa. As Assyria was wishing to enter the Med. Egypt brushed them back; but just for a few centuries. Of the different ownerships in the thirty-five centuries, Asilah is now an Art Town.

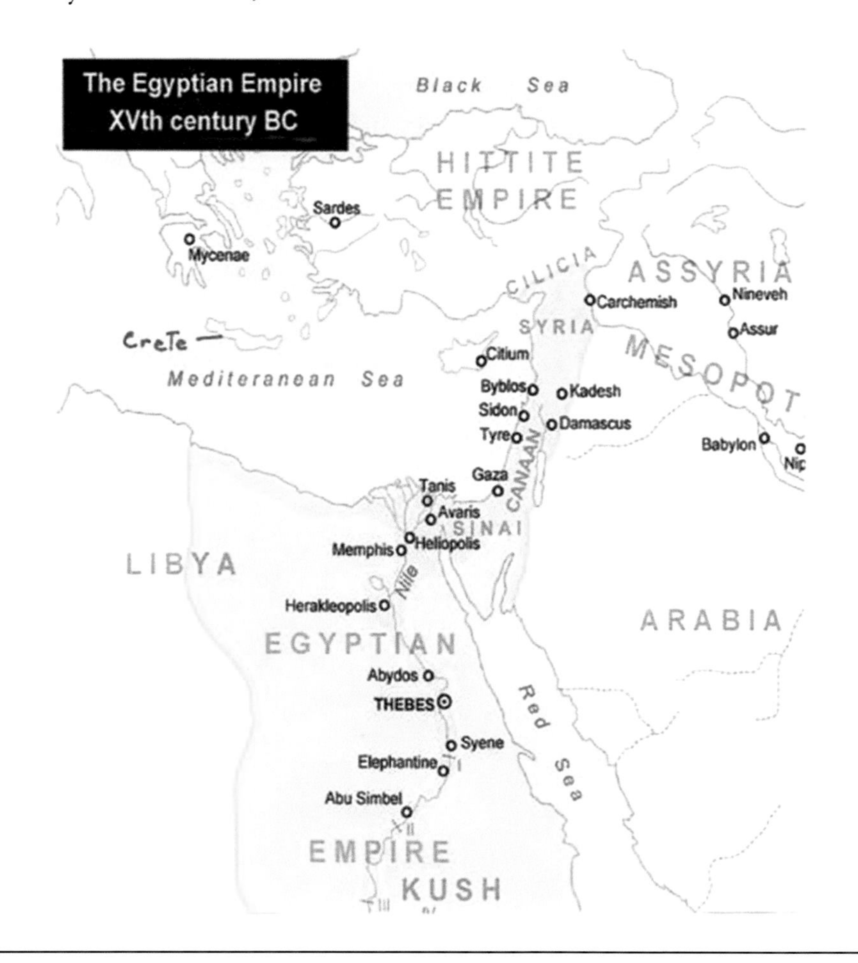

Our Wikipedia pictures of Chefchaouen and Asilah have brought us home – that is by time – and so, Tuesday morning in Volubilis. Before strolling back to the bus, there are two items that deserve note: "The ancient Greek philosopher Aristotle wrote extensively on Carthaginian Politics, and he considered their city to have one of the best governing institutions in the world, along with those of the Greek states of Sparta and Crete."

The second item is not a quote, but simply an observation by we all. Consider the countries that have enlarged themselves by becoming in charge of another country; owning it. It becomes more expensive with time. For how long did Rome own the Mediterranean? After beating Carthage in 146 BC, Rome became "One of the largest empires in the ancient world…until 395 – 476 AD Decline of the Western Roman Empire." Their relocation to Byzantine in 330 AD, and the great changes done by the Roman Emperor Constantine from 306 to 337 AD (ex: civil and military authority separated; a new gold coin; government was restructured. It would become the standard for Byzantine and Europe currencies for more than a thousand years.) That city was renamed Constantinople after his death.

Phoenician State thrived for three thousand years because they make, buy and sell with no baggage; just trade. And learn.

We drove a short distance to the city of Meknes. Ismail Ibn Sharif was born in 1634. He Reigned from 1672 – 1727. As he began, there were plenty of internal tribal wars and royal successions. He became known as the "Warrior King". Upon relocating the capital from Fes to the new Meknes, much of the removed stones of Volubilis are at Meknes. On the walls of the city can be seen ten thousand heads of those he displeased. He fought the Ottoman Turks in 1679, 1682, and 1695-96. After these battles, Moroccan independence was respected. He obviously allowed the Berbers to continue – to flourish – their capturing; no doubt a percentage to him.

We arrived only here at his stable.

Ismail Ibn Sharif

The capital he built is sometimes called the 'Versailles of Morocco' because of its extravagance. Ismail created The black Guard, black tribes brought from Sub-Sahran Africa who settled with their families in special Colonies at Mechra er Remel, to have children. At age 10, they were trained in certain skills; girls in domestic life or entertainments, and the boys in masonry, archery, horsemanship, and marketing. At age 15, those that were chosen entered the army. They would marry, have children and continue the cycle. Considered more loyal than Arab or Berber warriors. Ismail's black soldiers formed the bulk of his standing army of 150,000 at their peak.

"Collecting taxes, patrolling Morocco's unstable countryside; they crushed rebellions against Ismail's rule. Ismail always went about his court surrounded by a bodyguard of eighty black soldiers, with muskets and scimitars at the ready in case of any attempt on the sultan's life. It is estimated 30,000 people died under his rule."

Wikipedia

Page 75 mentions an earthquake in the mid-eighteenth century. It was indeed "A.D. 1755 when Volubilis, and more, Meknes were severely damaged. By 1757 Ismail's grandson Mohammad 111 moved the capita at Marrakech" – Wikipedia

As we exited Ismail Shariff's horse stable, we saw a horse racing track; just like the Arabian horses we watched run in Marrakech. While driving straight west on our way to Rabat we passed a farm making strictly cork – 130,000 Hecters (1 hecter = 2.5 acres). Next on our route west was the building titled African Money Exchange; unfortunately no stopping.

We soon arrived into Rabat.

"The Hassan Tower began in A.D. 1195, the tower was intended to be the largest minaret in the world along with the mosque, also intented to be the world's largest. In 1199 Sultan Yacoub Al-Mansour died and construction of mosque stopped. The tower reached 44m (140ft), about half of its intended height. Instead of stair, the tower is ascended by ramps. The minaret's ramps would have allowed the muezzin to ride a horse to the top of the tower to issue the call to prayer"

-Wikipedia

Completed in 1971

"The building is considered a masterpiece of modern Alaouite dynasty. Architecture, with its white silhouette, topped by typical green roof, green being the color of Islam". – Wikipedia

As entering this Mausoleum one can gaze at the resting of Mohammed V, and his two sons, King Hammers II, and Prince Abdalah.

Our first order of business this last day in Morocco was to go inside the Hassan II Mosque. I did discuss that back on page 8. One thing did not mention in regards of our first time at that Mosque – just walking around- was our observation to its north, was the great amount of construction going on; most building just doing the completion, all 20 floors minimum. One month later, this 4 page article from *Forbes* was presented: (actually a month before we were there in Nov.)

King Mohammed VI

King Mohammed VI Of Morocco Builds New Financial City For The World Ever since he ascended to the throne in 1999, his Majesty Mohammed VI, King of Morocco, has nursed one persistent ambition to transform Casablanca, the Kingdom's largest city and economic center, into Africa's leading financial hub.

To achieve this, in 2010 the King announced the creation of one of his most ambitious projects, the Casablanca Finance City (CFC), a regional financial center and a privileged entry point for Northern, Western, and Central Africa.

"The Casablanca Finance City (CFC) is a custom-made village being developed for large national and international foreign institutions looking to operate in a region and gain access to Frenchspeaking African markets. The city will cater primarily to institutions in 3 key sectors: financial services, professional services and national and international headquarters activities, offering eligible companies operating in these sectors a marketplace to undertake their activities on a regional and international level.

The CFC zone sits on 100 hectares "situated at the heart of Casablanca", but note: it is outside the area showing the cities history and a max number of floors.

"...companies from around the world are already applying for operating licenses. At the moment, more than 25 companies have obtained holding company controlled by Moroccan billionaire Othman Benjelloun, signed an agreement to construct his headquarter office in CFC."

"The CFC Head believes that Morocco stands out as the most logical option for a financial center because of socio-economic. Reasons including political stability within the regional context of agitation within the framework of the Arab spring, as well as strong historical lies with Africa, sustainable macroeconomic indicators and free trade agreements with the European Union, the United States and the Middle East. Morocco also has improved access to African markets through key agreements with African Countries"

http://www.forbes.com/sites/mFonobongselie/2013/10/16king-mohammed-vi-of-morocco....1/3/2014

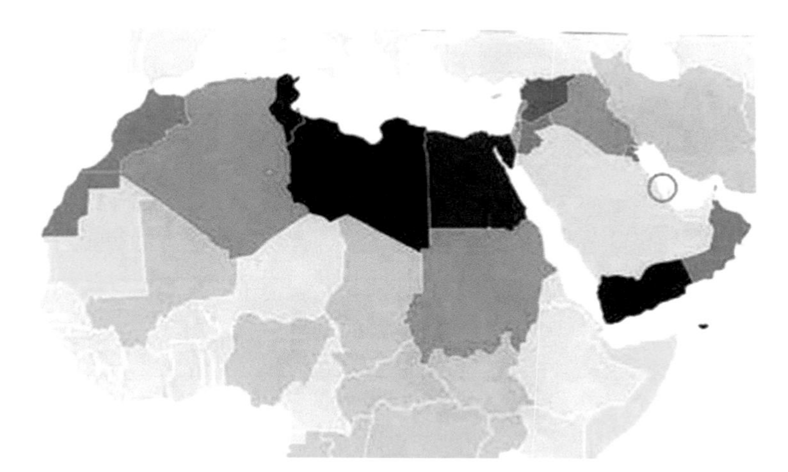

There were a few items not mentioned in this article of the New Financial City. Soon upon rising to the King's throne in 1999, Mohammed VI had several changes done for the ladies in jobs, equal laws; all of the farm owners were given new equipment for free, and then almost no tax to be given back for all sold. By the end of the first decade of the 21st Century, Morocco was listed as number one on olive oil. In our travel through Morocco, most hotels, restaurants, etc. had a picture of the King on the wall of the entrance. The so-called "Protests and Government changes" were not true to Morocco, for they were already given their freedom for protest long before A.D. 2011.

This is Ahmed

Ahmed, our bus no. 3 coach / mentor:
"A Man for all Seasons"

Printed in the United States
By Bookmasters